JOURNAL
OF
A RESIDENCE IN INDIA

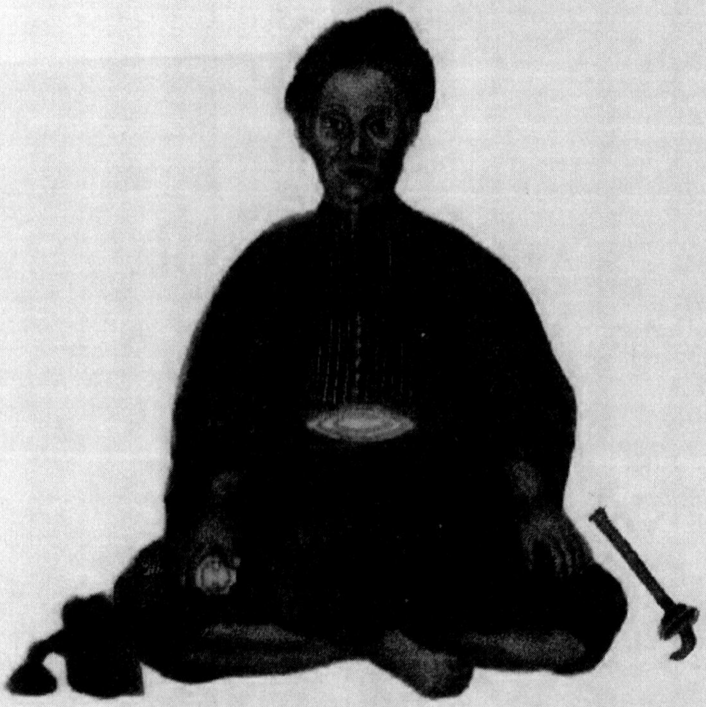

E. Mitchell sculp.

IBRAHIM A MALAY MOONSHEE

FROM A NATIVE DRAWING.

JOURNAL
OF
A RESIDENCE IN INDIA

BY

MARIA GRAHAM

ILLUSTRATED BY ENGRAVINGS.

SECOND-EDITION

GYAN

Published by

GYAN

Gyan Publishing House
5, Ansari Road
Daryaganj, New Delhi-110002
Phone: 011-47034999, 9811692060
E-mail: books@gyanbooks.com

Distribution Network
gyanbooks.com
India, USA, Canada, UK, Australia, France

ISBN : 978-81-212-3641-6 (PB)
First Published, London, 1812

2nd Impression 2020

Printed at: Gyan Press, Delhi.

Journal of A Residence in India
Author: Maria Graham

JOURNAL

OF

A RESIDENCE IN INDIA.

BY

MARIA GRAHAM.

ILLUSTRATED BY ENGRAVINGS.

EDINBURGH:
PRINTED BY GEORGE RAMSAY AND COMPANY,
FOR ARCHIBALD CONSTABLE AND COMPANY, EDINBURGH; AND
LONGMAN, HURST, REES, ORME, AND BROWN,
LONDON.

1812.

PREFACE.

Though India has certainly been visited by a greater number of intelligent Englishmen than any other foreign country, and has been the subject of innumerable publications, it is remarkable that there is no work in our language containing such a popular and comprehensive view of its scenery and monuments, and of the manners and habits of its natives and resident colonists, as we are commonly furnished with by travellers in countries incomparably less deserving of notice. The chief reason of this probably is, that few people go to this remote region as mere idle or philosophical observers; and that of the multitude of well-educated individuals who pass the best part of their days in it, the greater part are too constantly occupied with the cares and duties of their respective vocations as statesmen, soldiers, or traders, to pay much attention to what is merely curious or interesting to a contemplative spectator. Having for the most part, too, the prospect of a long residence, they rarely think, on their first arrival, of recording or digesting the impressions which they receive from the spectacle that is spread before them, and wait so long to mature and extend their information, that the interest of novelty is lost, and the scene becomes too familiar to seem any longer worth the trouble of a careful delineation. The fact accordingly is, that almost all our modern publications on the subject of India, are entirely occupied with its political and military history,—details and suggestions upon its trade and commercial resources,—and occasionally with discussions upon the more recondite parts of its literary or mythological antiquities. Notwithstanding the great number of these books, therefore, and the unquestionable excellence of many of them, there still seemed to be room for a more popular work on the subject of this great country,—a work which, without entangling its readers in the thorny walk of politics or commercial speculation, should bring before them much of what strikes the eye and the mind of an observant stranger,—and addressing itself rather to the general reader than to those who are professionally connected with the regions it describes, should perform the same humble but useful office as to India, which tolerably well written books of travels have done as to most of the other countries of the world.

This purpose it has been suggested to the writer of the following pages might be accomplished in some degree by their publication,—and it is with these, and with no higher pretensions, that they are now offered to the Public. They were really and truly written, nearly as they now appear, for the amusement of an intimate friend, and without the remotest view to the destiny they have now to encounter, having been prepared for publication merely by the omission of such private details and trifling anecdotes of individuals as could not with propriety be obtruded on the world. The writer is afraid that she secretly means this statement to be received as a kind of apology for some of their imperfections. But the truth is, that she is extremely doubtful whether she could have made the work much better by digesting it with more labour. Its merit, if it have any, must consist in the fidelity and liveliness of a transcript from new impressions,—and this she has found it would have been in great danger of losing, if she had ventured to change the character of her original sketch, by attempting (perhaps after all not very successfully), to reduce its redundancies or to strengthen its colouring.

In one particular she is sensible that the changes she has made in her original manuscript, have both lessened its authority and tasked her self-denial; she alludes to the obligation she has imposed upon herself, of suppressing the names of those individuals to whom she has been so greatly indebted both for kindness and information, but whom she does not think herself entitled to bring before the Public without their express permission. She may be allowed, however, to mention, that at Bombay, at Madras, and at Calcutta, she had the good fortune to be acquainted with many individuals distinguished for oriental learning and research, and that in their society she had opportunities of acquiring much information with regard to the civil and religious habits and opinions of the natives, which she must otherwise have sought in vain. How far she has availed herself of these advantages the Public must now judge; all she pretends to is the merit of a correct description of the scenery of the country, and, as far as her powers and opportunities permitted, a faithful delineation of the manners of the inhabitants.

It may be proper to add, that she went to India early in 1809, and the first months of her residence in that country were spent in Bombay, which, besides its importance as the third British presidency in India, is interesting from its neighbourhood to some of the most ancient and magnificent monuments of Hindoo art. Of these the cave of Elephanta is the most interesting, and perhaps it has been most frequently described. The island of Salsette is also rich in antiquities of the same kind, but it has attracted less notice; and the excavations of Carli, in the Mahratta mountains, are in comparison recently discovered. Curiosity induced her to visit all these places, and, when at the latter, to continue her journey to Poonah, the Mahratta capital. On her return to Bombay, she embarked for Ceylon, where she arrived at Pointe de Galle, and travelled along the coast as far as Negombo; afterwards visiting Trincomale on the east side of the island on her voyage to Madras. From Madras the writer went to Calcutta, which terminated her travels in India, as she only returned to the Coromandel coast to embark for England, in the beginning of 1811; where, after touching at the Cape of Good Hope and St Helena, she arrived in the summer of the same year.

With the exception of the town of Poonah and the visit to Calcutta, the Journal consequently only describes the country and the people immediately on the coast. This perhaps may account in some degree for her character of the natives being more unfavourable than that of some other writers; and most certainly she did not go far enough to meet with any of those remnants of the age of gold—any of those combinations of innocence, benevolence, and voluptuous simplicity, with which the imaginations of some ingenious authors have peopled the cottages of the Hindoos. What she saw certainly suggested the materials of a very opposite picture;—and, though aware that, among a people whose laws, whose religion, whose arts, whose habits of reasoning and notions of politeness, all differ from ours, as radically as their language or complexion, it was natural to expect some variation from our standards as to the morals and the charities and decencies of social life, she must confess that the difference was greater than she found it easy to reconcile to herself, even by these considerations. In the sketch which she has attempted to exhibit, therefore, of this singular people, she flatters herself that she may have afforded some entertainment, and some matter of useful meditation even to the reflecting reader; and ventures to hope that she may perhaps contribute, in some instances, to direct the attention of those in whose hands so much of their destiny is placed, to the means of improving their moral and intellectual condition, as well as of securing them from political or civil injuries.

ERRATA.

Page 10 line 24, *for* pine *read* fine
32 — 20, teak main-mast.—I have since learnt that the mast was of *poon*, and therefore lighter.
37 — 24, — fine *read* fire.
81 — 1, — enterprises *read* enterp rise
88 — 27, — Pupil *read* Peepil
125 note, *for* Hutopodesa *read* Heetopadesa
132 line 8, *for* Sangor *read* Saugor
135 — 25, — mogue *read* mogree
136 — 16, — Mahajah *read* Maharajah
139 — 1, — travellers, representations *read* travellers' representations
142 — 27, — port *read* park
154 — 4, — Sangor *read* Saugor
195 — 5, — Tehranu *read* Tehraun.

DIRECTIONS FOR PLACING THE PLATES.

M. G. del.

Etch'd by James Storer.

Temple of Maho Deo, in Bombay.

Publish'd July 1. 1812 by A. Constable & Co. Edinburgh.

JOURNAL

OF A

SHORT RESIDENCE IN INDIA.

Bombay, May 28, 1809.

MY DEAR FRIEND,

IN compliance with your parting request, that during my absence from England I would make notes and journals for you of whatever appeared to me worthy of remark, either as curious in itself, or as differing from the customs, manners, and habits of Europe, I shall endeavour faithfully to describe whatever I see, and carefully to report whatever I learn, for your amusement, warning you that I mean to paint from the life, and to adhere to the sober colouring of nature. After a voyage from England of twenty weeks, we landed here on the 26th of this month, in a thick fog, which presaged the coming on of the rainy-season in this part of India. On the new *bunder*, or pier, we found *palankeens* waiting to convey us from the shore. These palankeens are litters, in which one may either lie down or sit upright, with windows and sliding doors; the modern ones are little carriages, without wheels; those anciently used were of a different form, and consisted of a bed or sofa, over which was an arch just high enough to admit of sitting upright; it was decorated with gold or silver bells and fringes, and had a curtain to draw occasionally over the whole. The palankeen-bearers are here called *hamauls*, (a word signifying carrier); they for the most part wear nothing but a turban, and a cloth wrapped round the loins, a degree of nakedness which does not shock one, owing to the dark colour of the skin, which, as it is unusual to European eyes, has the effect of dress. These people come chiefly from the Mahratta country, and are of the *coombee* or agricultural caste. Their wages are seven or eight rupees a month; they are a hardy race, and, if trusted, honest, but otherwise they consider theft innocent, if not meritorious.

Leaving the bunder we crossed the esplanade, which presented a gay and interesting scene, being crowded with people in carriages, on horseback, and on foot. A painter might have studied all the varieties of attitude and motion in the picturesque figures of the *koolies* employed in washing at their appropriate *tanks* or wells which are numerous on the esplanade, each tank being surrounded by broad stones, where groupes of men and women are continually employed in beating the linen, while the better sort of native women, in their graceful costume, reminding one of antique sculptures, are employed in drawing, filling, or carrying water from the neighbouring wells. The Hindoo women wear a short boddice with half sleeves, which fastens behind, and is generally made of coloured brocade. The *shalie*, a long piece of coloured silk or cotton, is wrapped round the waist in form of a petticoat, which leaves part of one leg bare, while the other is covered to the ancle with long and graceful folds, gathered up in front, so as to leave one end of the shalie to cross the breast, and form a drapery, which is sometimes thrown over the head as a veil. The Mussulman and Parsee women have nearly the same clothing, in addition to which they wear long loose trowsers. The hair is drawn back from the face, where the roots are often stained red, and fastened in a knot behind. The hands and feet of the native women are in general delicately shaped, and are covered with rings and *bangles* or bracelets, which sometimes conceal the arm as far as the elbow, and the leg as far as the calf. As the food, lodging, and dress of the lower class of natives cost very little, it is common to see both the men and women adorned with massy rings and chains of gold and silver, round their necks, arms, waists, and legs, and the toes and fingers decked with fine filigree rings, while the ears and nose are hung with pearls or precious stones. The vanity of parents sometimes leads them to dress their children, even while infants, in this manner, which affords a temptation, not always resisted, to murder these helpless creatures for the sake of their ornaments or *joys*. The custom of laying out the whole, or at least the greater part of their wealth, in ornaments for the person, has probably arisen among the natives of India from the miserable state of society for so many ages. Where the people were daily exposed to the ravages of barbarous armies, it was natural to endeavour to keep their little wealth in that form in which it could with most ease be conveyed out of the reach of plunderers; for this purpose, jewels were certainly the best adapted; and though the necessity for the practice has in a great measure ceased, custom, which has perhaps more influence in India than in any other country, continues it.

On entering the Black Town, which is built in a coco-nut wood, I could not help remarking the amazing populousness of this small island; the streets appear so crowded with men, women, and children, that it seems impossible for the quiet bullock *hackrays*, or native carriages, to get along without doing mischief; much less the furiously driving coaches of the rich natives, who pride themselves upon the speed of their horses, which are more remarkable for beauty and for swiftness than for strength. I was informed that Bombay contains upwards of two hundred thousand inhabitants. The Europeans are as nothing in this number, the Parsees from six to eight thousand, the Mussulmans nearly the same number, and the remainder are Portuguese and Hindoos, with the exception of about three or four thousand Jews, who long passed in Bombay for a sect of Mahometans, governed by a magistrate called the cazy of Israel; they willingly eat and converse with the Mussulmans. A number of them are embodied among the marine sepoys, but most of them are low traders. The dwellings of the rich natives are surrounded by virandas, equally necessary to guard against the intemperate heat of the sun and the monsoon rains; they are generally painted in flowers and leaves of a green or red colour; those of the Hindoos have usually some of the fables of their mythology represented on their walls. The houses are necessarily of great extent, because, if a man has twenty sons, they all continue to live under the same roof even when married; and uncles, brothers, sons, and grandsons, remain together till the increase of numbers actually forces a part of the family to seek a new dwelling. The lower classes content themselves with small huts, mostly of clay, and roofed with *cadjan*, a mat made of the leaves of the Palmyra or coco-nut tree, plaited together. Some of these huts are so small, that they only admit of a man's sitting upright in them, and barely shelter his feet when he lies down. There is usually a small garden round each house, containing a few herbs and vegetables, a plantain tree and a coco-nut or two. The coco-nut is the true riches of a native Indian. The fruit forms a chief article of food during several months in the year, and from it the oil for the lamp is expressed, after being dried in the sun. The fibrous covering of the nut is steeped, and becomes like hemp, though more harsh; it is then called *coier*, and is used for making cordage of all kinds. The *tarry*, or toddy (which is a juice procured from the tree, by making an incision in the bark near the top, or cutting off one of the lower leaves, and applying an earthen pot to the aperture in the bark), when distilled, furnishes arrack; that which flows in the night is the sweetest, and, drank before sun-rise it is very wholesome. The leaves cover the houses, and two of them plaited together form a light basket-work cloak, which the peasants wear in the rainy season while transplanting the rice. When no longer capable of yielding fruit or tarry, the wood makes excellent water-pipes and joists and beams for houses. The *Palmyra*, another tree of the family of palms, here called the *brab*, furnishes the best leaves for thatching, and the dead ones serve for fuel. The trunk is applied to the same purposes as that of the coco-nut, and is said to resist the attacks of the white ant. The brab grows on hills and stony places. The coco requires a low sandy soil, and much water. In the outskirts of the Black Town we saw the fields already flooded for the rice; they are ploughed in this state; the plough consists of a piece of crooked stick which is drawn by an ox or a cow, or sometimes both. The buffaloes make good draught cattle, and are commonly used for drawing water; the other cattle are of the kind which has a hump on the shoulders; they are used by the natives to draw carriages called hackrays, to which they are only fastened by a beam, which is at the end of the pole, and lies across their necks ; they use no traces.

As there is but one tavern in Bombay, and as that is by no means fit for the reception of ladies, the hospitality of the British inhabitants is always exercised towards new-comers, till they can provide a place of residence for themselves. We have the good fortune to be under the hospitable roof of Sir James and Lady Mackintosh, at Tarala, about three miles from the fort and town of Bombay. Sir James possesses the best library that ever doubled the Cape; it is arranged in a large room like the cell of a temple, surrounded with a viranda inclosed by Venetian shutters, which admit and exclude the light and air at pleasure. As the apartment is at the top of the house, which is built on an eminence, it commands on all sides charming views; in short, it combines all the agrēmens that one can look for in a place of studious retirement, and we feel its value doubly from having been so long confined to the cabin of a frigate.

August 10*th.*—The rainy season, which began in the middle of May, still continues, but we have sometimes intervals of several days of dry fine weather, so that we have been able to visit most of the villages within the island of Bombay. The first walk we took was to Mazagong, a dirty Portuguese village, putting in its claim to Christianity, chiefly from the immense number of pigs kept there. It is beautifully situated on the shore between two hills, on one of which is Mazagong house, a leading mark into the harbour. It is interesting to the admirers of sentimental writings, as the house from which Sterne's Eliza eloped, and perhaps may call forth the raptures of some future pensive traveller, as strongly as the sight of Anjengo does those of the Abbé Raynal, when he remembers " that it is the birth place of Eliza." Mazagong has, however, more solid claims to attention; it has an excellent dock for small ships, and is adorned with two tolerably handsome Romish churches; but its celebrity in the East is owing to its mangoes, which are certainly the best fruit I ever tasted. The parent tree, from which all those of this species have been grafted, is honoured during the fruit season by a guard of sepoys; and in the reign of Shah Jehan, couriers were stationed between Dehli and the Mahratta coast, to secure an abundant and fresh supply of mangoes for the royal table.

Our next excursion was to Sion, nine miles from the fort of Bombay, and at the opposite extremity of the island. We drove through a country like an English park, where I first saw the banian, or Indian fig-tree. It is a large spreading tree, from the branches of which long fibres descend to the ground, and there taking root become new trunks, and thus spread over a very great space * The banian is sacred, and is usually to be found near the *Pagodas*, as the Europeans call the Hindoo temples. I have seen the natives walk round it in token of respect, with their hands joined, and their eyes fixed on the ground; they also sprinkle it with red and yellow dust, and strew flowers before it; and it is common to see at its root stones sculptured with the figures of some of the minor Hindoo gods. Sion Fort is on the top of a small conical hill; it commands the passage from Bombay to the

* See the Plate.

In the histories of Alexander's expedition to India, it is mentioned that the natives bent down the branches of the trees, which then took root and grew again. Is not this a description of the banian tree?

neighbouring island of Salsette, and was of importance while the Mahrattas possessed that island, but it now only serves to beautify the scene. It is manned with a few invalids, and commanded by General Macpherson, a Highlander, who was in the battle of Culloden, on the losing side, and who, at the age of forty, came to Bombay as a cadet in the Company's army. He retains so strong a recollection of his early years, that when the Culloden, with Sir Edward Pellew's flag, was in Bombay harbour, no entreaties could prevail on him to go on board of her,—he always shook his head, and said he had had enough of Culloden.

At the foot of the little hill of Sion is a causeway, or *vellard*, which was built by Mr Duncan, the present governor, across a small arm of the sea, which separates Bombay and Salsette. It is well constructed of stone, and has a draw-bridge in the middle, but it is too narrow for carriages to go along with safety in bad weather; however, it is of great advantage to the farmers and gardeners who bring in the daily supplies of provisions to the Bombay market. The vellard was begun A. D. 1797, and finished in 1805, at the expence of 50,575 rupees, as I learnt from an inscription over a small house at the end next Bombay, where a guard is kept to prevent the introduction of contraband articles from Salsette, which, though under the English government, is still subject to the Mahratta regulations with regard to taxes.

From Sion we went to Mahaim, passing in the way several neglected Portuguese churches, Mussulman tombs, and Hindoo temples, but nothing very interesting till we reached the coco-nut wood near the village, where there are two beautiful temples, with large tanks surrounded by trees. These tanks are the great luxuries of the natives; one sees people bathing in them from morning till night, all ages and sexes together; but they wear as much

M. G. del.^t Etch'd by James Storer.

Banian Tree.

Pub.^d by A. Constable & Co. Edinburgh June 1. 1812.

clothing in the water as out of it. There is at Mahaim a *Pir's kubber*, or Mussulman saint's tomb, with a fine mosque attached to it, both under the guardianship of a Mahometan family of the Sooni sect *. The Portuguese church at Mahaim is close to the sea, and is surrounded by trees. Attached to it there is a college for native Catholic priests; but those who pretend to learning, usually study at Goa, where they learn to speak barbarous Latin, and have the advantage of occasionally seeing priests from Europe. A small premium is given at the church for every native child who is baptized, consequently a number of Hindoo women present their offspring for that purpose, who never think farther of Christianity.

From Mahaim a good causeway leads to Parell, the governor's country house, which was formerly a Jesuits college. It is said that the holy fathers employed their penitents in the construction of this useful work.

August 15*th.*—A longer continuance of fine weather than usual tempted us yesterday to go to Malabar Point, at the south-west extremity of the island, formerly a place of singular sanctity, and where a number of pilgrims still annually resort. We left our carriage at the foot of the hill, and ascended a long flight of irregular steps to the top. Near the summit there are a multitude of small temples, and a few Bramins' houses, whose inhabitants generally beg from the passengers and strangers whom business or curiosity lead to the hill. After walking nearly two

* The Soonis and the Sheeas are the two Mahomedan sects most prevalent in India. The Soonis are the most numerous on this side of the peninsula; they are divided into Hunafis and Shafeis.

miles through gardens, or rather fields of vegetables, we came to a small *bungalo*, or garden-house, at the point of the hill, from which there is, I think, the finest view I ever saw. The whole island lay to the north and east, beautifully green with the young rice, varied with hills and woods, and only separated from Salsette and the Mahratta shore by narrow arms of the sea, while the bay and harbour to the south, scattered with beautiful woody islands, reflected the grand monsoon clouds, which, as they rolled along, now hid and now discovered the majestic forms of the ghauts on the main-land. Within a few yards of the bungalo is a ruined temple; from what remains, it must have been a fine specimen of Hindoo architecture; almost every stone is curiously carved with groupes of figures, animals, and other ornaments. Tradition says that the Portugueze, in their zeal for conversion, pointed cannon against this temple, and destroyed it with its gods; its widely scattered remains seem to countenance the report. Close to the ruin there is a cleft in a rock, so narrow, that one would wonder how a child could get through it, nevertheless, there are multitudes of pilgrims who annually come to force themselves through, as a certain method of getting rid of their sins.

Half a mile from the old temple I saw a most beautiful village, entirely inhabited by Bramins. In the centre is a large tank, on the banks of which are some pine trees and high pyramidical pillars, which are lighted up on festivals. A broad road round the tank separates it from the temples, which are more numerous than the houses; they are mostly dedicated to *Siva*, under the name of *Maha Deo*, and to his wife *Parvati*. The sacred bull *Nandi* is placed in front of all Siva's temples in Bombay, and I have generally observed a tortoise at his feet. The Bramins of this village speak and write English; the young men are mostly *parvoes*, or writers, and are employed in the public offices and merchants' counting-houses, while the elders devote themselves to their sacerdotal duties, and the study of the Vedas; but I am tempted to believe that the Bramins of Bombay are very ignorant, even with regard to their own sciences.

The road from Malabar Hill to the Fort of Bombay lies along the beach of Back-bay, a dangerous bay formed by the point of Malabar on one side, and by Old Woman's Island, or Coulaba, on which is the light-house, on the other. The shore is the general burial-place of all classes of inhabitants. That of the English is walled in and well kept; it is filled with pretty monuments, mostly of chunam, and contains many an unread inscription, sacred to the memory of those who, to use the oriental style, "had "scarcely entered the garden of life, much less had they gathered "its flowers." Next to the British cemetery is that of the Portuguese, after which follow those of the Armenians, the Jews, and the Mahomedans, with the few Hindoos who bury their dead, in regular succession; they are all overshadowed by a thick coco-nut wood, and the ride among the monuments, placed between the grove and the sea, would be far from unpleasing, were it not that the tide continually washes in the skulls and bones of the Hindoos who are burnt on the beach at low water. After passing the burying-grounds, we saw several pretty country-houses along the sea-shore, as we approached the esplanade in our way to the fort.

The Fort of Bombay is said to be too large to be defended, if ever an European enemy should effect a landing on the island, and no part of it is bomb-proof; besides which, the native houses within the walls are closely crowded together, very high, and mostly built of wood. The fort is dirty, hot, and disagreeable, particularly the quarter near the bazar-gate, owing to the ruins of houses which were burnt down some time ago, and have never been removed; but new buildings are in many places rising on the broken fragments of the old, so that the streets are become so uneven as to render it disagreeable, if not dangerous, for carriages to pass through them. The most important and interesting object in the fort is the dock-yard, where a new dock is nearly finished, consisting of two basons, in the inner one of which there is already a seventy-four gun ship on the stocks. The old dock is still serviceable, though much out of repair, and too small to admit a large ship; it was found a few inches too short to receive the Blenheim, so that she could not receive the repairs she required previous to her leaving India. The new dock is said to be complete and excellent in its kind; it is the work of Captain Cooper of the Company's engineers. There is a steam-engine for pumping it dry, as it is sunk too low to be left dry by the tide at any season. Bombay is the only place in the East where the rise of tide is sufficient to construct docks on a large scale, the highest spring-tides having never been known to be above seventeen feet, and rarely more than fourteen. The docks are the Company's property, and the King pays a high monthly rent for every ship taken into them. Near them is the castle, now used as an arsenal; it belongs to the King, and the governor of Bombay is also styled the governor of the King's castle of Bombay. The harbour is filled with vessels from all nations, and of all shapes, but the largest and finest of the foreigners are the Arabs. Our trade with them consists in horses, pearls, coffee, gums of various kinds, honey, and *ghee*, which is butter clarified and put into leathern jars. Besides these articles from Arabia, the Persian Gulf also furnishes dried fruits, ottur of roses, tobacco, rose-water, a small quantity of Schiraz wine, with a few articles of curiosity and luxury, as books, worked slippers, and silk shawls. The principal export from Bombay is raw cotton, which is chiefly drawn from the subject province of Guzerat, which likewise supplies us with wheat, rice, and cattle, besides vessels of earthen ware and metal for cooling liquors, carnelians, and other rare stones. The Laccadive and Maldive islands furnish the greatest quantity of coco-nuts for oil and coier for cordage; and from the forests of Malabar we get timber and various drugs and gums, particularly the Dammar, which is used here for all the purposes of pitch. In return for these things, we furnish British manufactures, particularly hardware, and a variety of Chinese articles, for which Bombay is the great depôt on this side of India.

While in the fort, we went to see the *screwing-houses*, where the bales of cotton are packed to go on board ship. The presses consist of a square frame, in which the cotton is placed, and a large beam of great weight, which is fixed to the end of a powerful screw. This screw is worked by a capstan, in a chamber above, to each bar of which there are often thirty men, so that there would be about two hundred and forty to each screw. They turn the screw with great swiftness at first, shouting the whole time, the shouts ending in something like loud groans, as the labour becomes heavier. Hemp is packed in the same manner, but it requires to be carefully laid in the press, for the fibres are apt to break if they are bent.

The only English church is in the fort; it is large, but neither well served nor attended. The Portuguese and Armenian churches are numerous, both within and without the walls, and there are three or four synagogues, and mosques and temples innumerable. The largest pagoda in Bombay is in the Black Town, about a mile and a half from the fort. It is dedicated to *Momba Devee*, or the Bombay goddess, who, by her images and attributes, seems to be Parvati, the wife of Siva. Within a large square, inclosed by high walls, there is a beautiful tank, well built of freestone, with steps to accommodate the bathers, according to the height of the water. Round the tank are houses for the Bramins, choultries for the reception of travellers, and temples to a variety of deities. One of these contains a well carved *trimurti*, or three formed god; it is a colossal bust with three faces, or rather three heads joined together; the centre represents Brahma the creator, the face on the right hand Siva the destroyer, and that on the left Vishnu the preserver. Offerings of rice, fruit, milk, and flowers, are daily made to these deities, and they are constantly sprinkled with water. The priests are of an olive complexion, being very little exposed to the sun; their dress consists of a linen scarf wrapped round the loins, and reaching nearly to the ancles, whose folds fall very gracefully: their heads are shaved, excepting the crown, where a small lock of hair is left; and over the shoulder hangs the braminical thread or zenaar. The zenaar must be made by a Bramin; it is composed of three cotton threads, each ninety-six cubits, (forty-eight yards) long. These are twisted together, then folded in three, and again twisted; after which it is folded in three again without twisting, and a knot made at each end; it is put over the left shoulder, and hangs down upon the right thigh. The Bramins assume it with great ceremony at seven years old, the Xetries at nine, and the Vaisyas at eleven. In the English settlements, when the Bramins go out of their houses, they usually put on the turban and the Mussulman jamma or gown. I saw at Momba Devee's temple some soi-disant holy men; they were young and remarkably fat, sprinkled over with ashes, and their hair was matted and filthy. I believe they had no clothing, for, during the few minutes I remained in the temple, they held a veil before them, and stood behind the Bramins. My expectations of Hindoo innocence and virtue are fast giving way, and I fear that, even among the Pariahs, I shall not find any thing like St Pierre's Chaumiere Indienne. In fact, the Pariahs are outcasts so despicable, that a Bramin not only would refuse to instruct them, but would think himself contaminated by praying for them. These poor creatures are employed in the lowest and most disgusting offices; they are not permitted to live in any town or village, or to draw water from the same well as the Hindoos. It is therefore not to be wondered at, that their minds are degraded in proportion to their personal situation. Near every Hindoo village there is commonly a hamlet of Pariahs, whose inhabitants pay a small tax to the *kalkurny*, or village-collector, for permission to reside near a bazar and wells, and they earn a subsistence by acting as porters and scavengers. They are filthy in all their habits, and do not scruple to use as food any dead animal they find; it is even said that, in some places, they do not reject human bodies *.

September 19th 1809.—We have spent our forenoon to-day very agreeably, in conversing with two well-informed natives, one a Hindoo, the other a Mussulman. They both speak English well, and are thoroughly informed in all that concerns the laws, reli-

* Thevenot says, that, when he was in India, (A. D. 1665), human flesh was publicly sold in the market at Debca, about forty leagues from Baroche.

gion, and customs of their own nations. The Pundit Bapoogee is a Brahmin of the Vedanti sect; he seems to take pleasure in giving us information concerning the mythology of the country, though he is very careful to convince us that he is superior to the belief of the popular superstitions, which he affects to deride as inventions to keep the lower classes of society, or, as he calls them, the *inferior castes*, in subjection. He is a man of about twenty-two years of age, elegant in his person and manners, and has an uncommon share of shrewdness and quickness of perception. I find him of the greatest use in explaining the customs, prejudices, and belief of his countrymen, and, in return, I do not find it very easy to satisfy his curiosity respecting England, to which country he has a great desire to travel, were it not for the fear of losing caste, or rather the privileges and honours attached to his own.

Our Mussulman friend, the Cazy Shahab o'dien Mahary, is a sincere Mahometan, and therefore a great bigot; however, he sometimes drinks tea with us, and does not scruple to eat bread, pastry, and fruit in our house. He is only two or three years older than Bapoogee, and though I doubt if his natural parts are so good, he is, I believe, a man of more learning; his manners are correct and gentleman-like, but not so refined as those of his Hindoo friend. He accompanied us the other day to several mosques in the neighbourhood, but, as they only differ from each other in size, I shall content myself with describing the largest. It is a square building, capable of containing five or six hundred people, supported by highly pointed arches, finished with cinquefoil heads, in rows from the front, which is open. The only interior ornament is a plain stone pulpit, for the imaum; the outside is adorned with carved work like that of the Gothic style.

The whole building is raised on arches over a large tank of excellent water, and surrounded by a paved court, in which there are a few tombs. Attached to each mosque there is a school where Arabic is taught; the master only attending to the elder boys, while the others are taught by their more advanced school-fellows; instead of books, there are alphabets and sentences painted on wood for the younger scholars.

My sister and I paid a visit to Shahab o'dien's harem, but could by no means prevail on the cazy to admit any of the gentlemen of our family. In the lower part of his house we saw a number of Mussulmans sitting cross-legged, with cushions at their backs, in the different apartments, perfectly idle, and rarely even speaking, and seeming hardly able to exert themselves so far as to put the betel into their mouths. We ascended to the women's apartment by a ladder, which is removed when not in immediate use, to prevent the ladies from escaping, and were received by the cazy's wife's mother, a fine old woman dressed in white, and without any ornaments, as becomes a widow. Shahab o'dien's mother, and the rest of his father's widows, were first presented, then Fatima his wife, to whom our visit was paid, and afterwards his sisters, some of them fine lively young women. They all crowded round us to examine our dress, and the materials of which it was composed. They were surprised at our wearing so few ornaments, but we told them it was the custom of our country, and they replied that it was good. I was not sorry that they so openly expressed their curiosity, as it gave us a better opportunity of gratifying our own. The apartment in which we were received was about twenty feet square, and rather low; round it were smaller rooms, most of them crowded with small beds, with white muslin curtains; these were not particularly clean, and the whole suite seemed close and disagreeable. Most of the women were becomingly dressed. Fatima's arms, legs, and neck, were covered with rings and chains; her fingers and toes were loaded with rings; her head was surrounded with a fillet of pearls, some strings of which crossed it several ways, and confined the hair, which was knotted up behind. On her forehead hung a cluster of coloured stones, from which depended a large pearl, and round her face small strings of pearl hung at equal distances. Her ear-rings were very beautiful; but I do not like the custom of boring the hem of the ear, and studding it all round with joys, nor could even Fatima's beautiful face reconcile me to the nose-jewel. Her large black eyes, the *cheshme ahoo* of the eastern poets, were rendered more striking by the black streaks with which they were adorned and lengthened out at the corners, and the palms of her hands, the soles of her feet, and her nails, were stained with *hinna*, a plant, the juice of whose seeds is of a deep red colour.

Fatima's manner is modest, gentle, and indolent; before her husband she neither lifts her eyes nor speaks, and hardly moves without permission from the elder ladies of the harem. She presented us with perfumed sherbet, fruit, and sweetmeats, chiefly made of ghee, poppy-seeds, and sugar; some of them were tolerably good, but it required all my good manners to swallow others. Prepared as I was to expect very little from Mussulman ladies, I could not help being shocked to see them so totally void of cultivation as I found them. They mutter their prayers, and some of them read the koran, but not one in a thousand understands it. Still fewer can read their own language, or write at all, and the only work they do is a little embroidery. They thread beads, plait coloured threads, sleep, quarrel, make pastry, and chew betel, in the same daily round; and it is only at a death, a birth, or a marriage, that the monotony of their lives is ever interrupted. When I took leave, I was presented with flowers and *paung*, (chunam and betel-nut wrapped in the leaf of an aromatic plant,) and sprinkled with rose-water.

As visits in the East are matters of ceremony, not of kindness, they are considered as a burden on the visitor, from which the person visited relieves him, as soon as he is satisfied with his company, by ordering refreshments, or offering the paung, which is a signal to depart. The highest affront one can offer to an Oriental, is to refuse his betel. Bernier tells a story of a young noble, who, to prove his loyalty, took and swallowed the paung from Shâh Jehan, though he knew it to be poisoned.

October 20th.—Having gone through the ceremony of receiving and returning the visits of all the ladies of the settlement, I have had an opportunity of seeing most of the European houses; and as I think our own the most agreeable residence I have seen, I shall content myself with a description of it, in order to give an idea of an Indian dwelling. It is pleasantly situated on the side of a hill, on the west side of Bombay, and commands a view of the greatest part of the island. On the summit are the ruins of a bungalo, once inhabited by Ragabhoy, during his exile from Poonah, which, with the clefts in the surrounding rocks, afford shelter to a few half-starved hyenas, who do no other mischief than stealing poultry and kids, and to innumerable jackalls, whose barking in the night is the greatest, I had almost said the only, inconvenience we feel here as to situation. The bases of the rocks are conçealed by the wood, which reaches quite down to the plain, and is composed of the brab, the tamarind, and mango trees, while here and there a little space is cleared for a garden, in which there are usually two or three gardeners houses. In our walk last night, we discovered one of these little hill colonies, which had till then escaped our observation. We found, at the principal hut, three very pretty children playing round their grandmother, who was sitting on the ground in a little viranda at the end of the house, grinding rice for the evening meal of the family. The mill consists of two round flat stones, in the lower one of which there is a groove to let out the flour; the middle of the upper one is inserted into a hollow in the other, and is turned by a wooden peg stuck into it, about one-third of the diameter from the edge. Three or four goats, with their kids, were tied to stakes round the door, and a few fowls were running about in the garden. We sat by the old woman while she made her bread, but at a sufficient distance not to pollute her cooking utensils or her fire. Every vessel she used, though apparently clean before, she carefully washed, and then mixed her rice-flour with milk, water, and salt, when she beat it between the palms of her hands till it was round and thin, and baked it on a round iron plate, such as is used in Scotland for oat-cakes. Besides these cakes, she prepared a few heads of maize, by rubbing off the chaff and laying them in the fire to roast for the family supper. At the next hut, the woman was grinding missala or curry stuff, on a flat smooth stone, with another shaped like a rolling-pin. Less than an English halfpenny procures enough of turmeric, spice, salt, and ghee, to season the whole of the rice eaten in a day by a labourer, his wife, and five or six children; the vegetables and acids he requires are found in every hedge. The curry was cooked with as much cleanliness as the bread, and the inside of both the huts was beautifully neat. In one corner in each, a large stone, with red powder sprinkled on it, stood as a household god, and before it were laid a few grains of rice and a coco-nut as offerings.

But to return to the description of the house. You enter it at one end of a viranda, which goes round four sides of a large square hall where we dine; on each side of the inner apartment are large glass doors and windows, so that we can admit or exclude the air as we please. The viranda keeps off the too great glare of the sun, and affords a dry walk during the rainy season. It is about twenty feet wide, and one side of it is one hundred feet long; the roof is supported by low arches, which are open to the garden. At one angle of the square formed by the viranda is the drawing-room, which has likewise a viranda on three sides, the fourth having a large bow-window overlooking the garden. The offices are connected with the house by a covered passage, and are concealed by thick shrubbery. Most of the country-houses in Bombay have but one story; ours has two. The bed-rooms above are well lighted and aired, and have glass windows within the Venetian shutters, which are only used in the rainy season, or during the land winds, which are cold and dry, and are said to give rheumatisms and cramps, with swelling, if they blow upon one while sleeping. Our garden is delightful; the walks are cut in the wood on the side of the hill, and covered with small sea-shells from the beach of Back Bay, instead of gravel, which, besides the advantage of drying quickly in the rainy season, are said to keep off snakes, whose skins are easily wounded by the sharp edges of the broken shells. On each side of the walks are ledges of brick, chunamed over, to prevent them from being destroyed by the monsoon rains. We are always sheltered from the sun by the fan-like heads of the palmyras, whose tall columnar stems afford a free passage to the air, and serve to support an innumerable variety of parasite and creeping plants, which decorate their rough bark with the gayest hues, vying with the beautiful shrubs which flourish beneath, and affording shelter to birds more beautiful than themselves. Some of these build in the sweet-scented champaka and the mango; and one, small as the humming-bird, fixes its curious nest to the pointed tips of the palmyra leaf, to secure its young from the tree-snake, while flights of paroquets daily visit the fruit-trees, and with their shrill voices hail the rising sun, joined by the *mina*, the kokeela, and a few other birds of song.

At the lowest part of the garden is a long broad walk, on each side of which grow vines, pamplemousses, figs, and other fruits, among which is the jumboo, a species of rose-apple, with its flowers, like crimson tassels, covering every part of the stem. Our grapes are excellent, but we are obliged to make an artificial winter for them, to prevent the fruit from setting at the beginning of the rainy season, which would destroy it. Every leafy branch is cut off, and nothing is left but the stump, and one or two leading branches; the roots are then laid bare and dry for three or four weeks, at the end of which a compost of fish, dead weeds, and earth, is heaped round them, the holes filled up, and the plants daily watered.

At one end of this walk are chunam seats, under some fine spreading trees, with the fruit-walk to the right hand, and to the left flower-beds filled with jasmine, roses, and tuberoses, while the plumbago rosea, the red and white ixoras, with the scarlet wild mulberry, and the oleander, mingle their gay colours with the delicate white of the moon-flower and the mogree. The beauty and fertility of this charming garden is kept up by constant watering from a fine well near the house. The water is raised by

1

a wheel worked by a buffalo; over the wheel two bands of rope pass, to each of which are tied earthen pots, about three or four feet from each other, which dip into the water as the wheel turns them to the bottom, and empty themselves as they go round, into a trough, communicating with chunam canals, leading to reservoirs in different parts of the garden. In short, this would be a little paradise, but for the reptiles peculiar to the climate. One of them, a white worm of the thickness of a fine bobbin, gets under the skin, and grows to the length of two or three feet. Dr Kier thinks the eggs are deposited in the skin by the wind and rain, as they are seldom found to attack those who never expose their legs or feet to the external air, and generally appear in the rainy monsoon. If they are suffered to remain in the flesh, or if they are broken in taking out, they occasion unpleasant sores. The native barbers extract them very dexterously with a sharp pointed instrument, with which they first remove the skin, then gradually dig till they seize the animal's head, which they fasten to a quill, round which they roll the worm, drawing out eight or nine inches daily, till the whole is extracted.

Snakes, from the enormous rock-snake, who first breaks the bones of his prey, by coiling round it, and then swallows it whole, to the smallest of the venomous tribe, glide about in every direction. Here the cobra-capella, whose bite is in almost every instance mortal, lifts his graceful folds, and spreads his large many-coloured crests; here too lurks the small bright speckled cobra-manilla, whose fangs convey instant death *.

* Some experiments were tried on wild dogs exposed to the bite of the cobra-manilla. Their ears were pressed between two boards, and the tips then presented to the snake, who bit them; the parts were cut off as expeditiously as possible, but the dogs died in a few seconds.

November 3.—The weather is now extremely pleasant; the mornings and evenings are so cool, that we can take long walks, but the middle of the day is still too hot to venture into the sunshine. The vegetable fields are in great beauty; I saw last night at least two acres covered with brinjaal, a species of solanum; the fruit is as large as a baking pear, and is excellent either stewed or broiled; the natives eat it plain boiled, or made into curry. The *bendy*, called in the West Indies *okree*, is a pretty plant, resembling a dwarf holyhock; the fruit is about the length and thickness of one's finger; it has five long cells full of round seeds. When boiled, it is soft and mucilaginous, and is an excellent ingredient in soups, curries, and stews, though I prefer it plain boiled. All sorts of gourds and cucumbers are in great plenty, but this is early in the season for them. Several plants produce long pods, which being cut small, are so exactly like French beans, that one cannot discover the difference, and they are plentiful all the year round, as are spinach, and a kind of cress which is boiled as greens. The common and sweet potatoes are excellent; but our best vegetable is the onion, for which Bombay is famous throughout the East. The peas and beans are indifferent, and the cabbage, carrots, and turnips, from European seed, are still scarce; sallad, parsley, and other pot-herbs, are raised in baskets and boxes in cool shady places, but celery thrives well, and is blanched by placing two circular tiles round the root. Twenty years ago the potatoe was scarcely known in India; but it is now produced in such abundance, that the natives in some places make considerable use of it. Bombay is supplied chiefly with this ex-

The eau de luce has sometimes cured the bite of the cobra-capella, but I have seen it fail, though applied within five minutes of the time of the bite.

cellent root from Guzerat, which province also furnishes us with wheat. The bread is the best I ever tasted, both for whiteness and lightness; the last quality it owes to being fermented with coco-nut toddy, no other being equal for that purpose. A little cheese is made in Guzerat, but it is hard and ill-flavoured, though the milk of the Guzerat cattle is very good, and yields excellent butter. The market at Bombay is mostly supplied with buffalo milk and butter; the latter article is insipid, and has a greenish hue, not very inviting to strangers. Our beef is tolerably good, though not fat; immediately after the rains, that of the buffalo is the best, though its appearance is unfavourable before it is dressed, and Europeans are in general strongly prejudiced against it. The mutton we get in the bazar is lean and hard, but either Bengal or Mahratta sheep, fed for six or eight weeks, furnish as good meat as one finds in the English markets. The kid is always good, and the poultry both good and abundant. The fish is excellent, but the larger kinds are not very plentiful. The *bumbelo* is like a large sand-eel; it is dried in the sun, and is usually eaten at breakfast with *kedgeree*, a dish of rice boiled with *dol* (split country peas), and coloured with turmeric. The prawns are the finest I ever saw, of an excellent flavour, and as large as craw-fish; they are frequently shelled, pressed flat, and dried. The island is too small to furnish much game, but the red-legged partridge is not uncommon, and we sometimes see snipes. Among other articles of food, I ought to mention frogs, which are larger here than I ever saw them, and are eaten by the Chinese and Portuguese, but not, I believe, by any of the other inhabitants of Bombay.

The lower classes of natives drink a great deal of arrack and *bhang*, an intoxicating liquor made from hempseed; there is also a strong spirit extracted from a kind of berry which I have not seen, called Parsee brandy; it has a strong burnt taste, which I think particularly disagreeable, but of which the people are very fond.

The other evening I followed a pretty child into a hut, where I found a native still at work. It is simply constructed. Round a hole in the earth, a ledge of clay, four inches high, is raised, with an opening about half a foot wide, for the purpose of feeding the fire. Upon the clay a large earthen pot is luted; to its mouth is luted the mouth of a second pot; and where they join, an earthen spout, a few inches long, is inserted, which serves to let off the spirit condensed in the upper jar, which is kept cool by a person pouring water constantly over it. When I went into the cottage, I found a woman sitting with a child in one arm, and with the other she cooled the still, pouring the water from a coco-nut shell ladle. She told me that she sat at her occupation from sunrise till sunset, and scarcely changed her position. While I was talking to her, her husband came home laden with toddy for distilling. He is a *bandari*, or toddy-gatherer. On his head was the common gardener's bonnet, resembling in shape the cap seen on the statues and gems of Paris, and called, I believe, the Phrygian bonnet; and at his girdle hung the implements of his trade. It is curious to see these people climbing the straight stems of the palms. Having tied their ancles loosely together, they pass a band round the tree and round their waist, and, placing their feet to the root of the tree, they lean upon the band, and with their hands and feet climb nimbly up a tree without branches, fifty feet high, carrying with them a bill or hatchet to make fresh incisions, or to renew the old ones, and a jar to bring down the toddy, which is received in a pot tied to the tree, and emptied every twelve hours.

Before I left the cottage, its inhabitants dressed themselves in their finest jewels, for the purpose of attending a marriage. I accompanied them a little way to join the procession, which at a distance looked like the groupes we see on antique bas-reliefs; in short, I every day find some traces of the manners and simplicity of the antique ages; but the arts and the virtues that adorned them are sunk in the years of slavery under which the devoted Hindoos have bent; these people, if they have the virtues of slaves, patience, meekness, forbearance, and gentleness, have their vices also. They are cunning, and incapable of truth; they disregard the imputations of lying and perjury, and would consider it folly not to practise them for their own interest. But,

> ————————— where
> Easily canst thou find one miserable,
> And not enforc'd oft-times to part from truth,
> If it may stand him more in stead to lie,
> Say, and unsay, fawn, flatter, or abjure?
>
> PAR. REG. B. i. l 470.

With regard to the Europeans in Bombay, the manners of the inhabitants of a foreign colony are in general so well represented by those of a country town at home, that it is hopeless to attempt making a description of them very interesting. However, as it may be gratifying to know how little there is to satisfy curiosity, I shall endeavour to describe our colonists. On our arrival we dined with the governor, and found almost all the English of the settlement invited to meet us. There were a good many very pretty and very well dressed women, a few ancient belles, and at least three men for every woman. When dinner was announced, I, as the stranger, though an unmarried woman, was handed by the governor into a magnificent dining-room, formerly the chapel of the Jesuits college, at one end of which a tolerable band was stationed to play during dinner We sat down to table about eight o'clock, in number about fifty, so that conversation, unless with one's next neighbour, was out of the question. After dinner, I was surprised that the ladies sat so long at the table; at length, after everybody had exhibited repeated symptoms of weariness, one of the ladies led the way into the saloon, and then I discovered that, as the stranger, I was expected to move first. Does not this seem a little barbarous? I found our fair companions like the ladies of all the country towns I know, under-bred and over-dressed, and, with the exception of one or two, very ignorant and very grossière. The men are, in general, what a Hindoo would call of a higher caste than the women; and I generally find the merchants the most rational companions. Having, at a very early age, to depend on their own mental exertions, they acquire a steadiness and sagacity which prepare their minds for the acquisition of a variety of information, to which their commercial intercourse leads.

The civil servants to government being, in Bombay, for the most part young men, are so taken up with their own imaginary importance, that they disdain to learn, and have nothing to teach. Among the military I have met with many well-informed and gentleman-like persons, but still, the great number of men, and the small number of rational companions, make a deplorable prospect to one who anticipates a long residence here.

8

The parties in Bombay are the most dull and uncomfortable meetings one can imagine. Forty or fifty persons assemble at seven o'clock, and stare at one another till dinner is announced, when the ladies are handed to table, according to the strictest rules of precedency, by a gentleman of a rank corresponding to their own. At table there can be no general conversation, but the different couples who have been paired off, and who, on account of their rank, invariably sit together at every great dinner, amuse themselves with remarks on the company, as satirical as their wit will allow; and woe be to the stranger, whose ears are certain of being regaled with the catalogue of his supposed imperfections and misfortunes, and who has the chance of learning more of his own history than in all probability he ever knew before. After dinner the same topics continue to occupy the ladies, with the addition of lace, jewels, intrigues, and the latest fashions; or if there be any newly-arrived young women, the making and breaking matches for them furnish employment for the ladies of the colony till the arrival of the next cargo. Such is the company at an English Bombay feast. The repast itself is as costly as possible, and in such profusion that no part of the table-cloth remains uncovered. But the dinner is scarcely touched, as every person eats a hearty meal called tiffin, at two o'clock, at home. Each guest brings his own servant, sometimes two or three; these are either Parsees or Mussulmans. It appears singular to a stranger to see behind every white man's chair a dark, long bearded, turbaned gentleman, who usually stands so close to his master, as to make no trifling addition to the heat of the apartment; indeed, were it not for the *punka*, (a large frame of wood covered with cloth), which is suspended over every table, and kept constantly swinging, in order to freshen the air, it would scarcely be possible to sit out the melancholy ceremony of an Indian dinner.

On leaving the eating-room, one generally sees or hears, in some place near the door, the cleaning of dishes, and the squabbling of cooks for their perquisites. If they are within sight, one perceives a couple of dirty Portuguese (black men who eat pork and wear breeches) directing the operations of half a dozen still dirtier Pariahs, who are scraping dishes and plates with their hands, and then, with the same unwashen paws, putting aside the next day's tiffin for their master's table.

The equipage that conveys one from a party, if one does not use a palankeen, is curious. The light and elegant figure of the Arab horses is a strong contrast with the heavy carriages and clumsy harness generally seen here; the coachman is always a whiskered Parsee, with a gay coloured turban, and a muslin or chintz gown, and there are generally two *massalgees*, or torch-bearers, and sometimes two horse-keepers, to run before one. On getting home, one finds a *sepoy* or *peon* walking round the open virandas of the house, as a guard. We have four of these servants, two of whom remain in the house for twenty-four hours, when they are relieved by the two others. These men carry messages, go to market, and attend to the removal of goods or furniture, but will carry nothing themselves heavier than a small book. The female servants are Portuguese, and they only act as ladies-maids, all household work being done by men, as well as the needle-work of the family.

The *derdjees*, or taylors, in Bombay, are Hindoos of a respectable caste, who wear the zenaar. My derdjee, a tall good-looking young man, wears a fine worked muslin gown, and a red or purple turban bordered with gold. He works and cuts out beautifully, making as much use of his toes as of his fingers in the last operation; his wages are fourteen rupees a-month, for which he works eight hours a-day; inferior workmen receive from eight to twelve rupees. Besides the hamauls for the palankeens, we have some for household-work; they make the beds, sweep and clean the rooms and furniture, and fetch water; on any emergency they help the palankeen-bearers, and receive assistance from them in return. For the meaner offices we have a Hallalcor or Chandela, (one of the most wretched Pariahs), who attends twice a-day. Two Massalgees clean and light the lamps and candles, and carry torches before us at night. One of these is a Pariah, so that he can clean knives, remove bones and rubbish, which his fellow-servant Nersu, who is of a good caste, will not do. Nersu fetches bread and flour, carries messages, and even parcels, provided they be not large enough to make him appear like a kooli or porter, and takes the greatest share of preparing the lamps, which are finger-glasses or tumblers half filled with water, on which they pour the coco-nut oil, always calculating it exactly to the number of hours the lamp has to burn; the wick is made of cotton twisted round a splinter of bamboo. The native masons, carpenters, and blacksmiths, are remarkably neat and dexterous in their several trades. There is plenty of stone on the island for building, but a good deal of brick is used. All the lime here is made from shells; it is called *chunam*, of which there are many kinds, one of which the natives eat with the betel-nut. They are very particular in gathering the shells, no person taking two different sorts; they are burnt separately, and it is said that the chunam varies according to the shell it is made from.

The Indian carpenter's tools are so coarse, and the native wood is so hard, that one would wonder that the work was ever performed. Almost every thing is done with a chissel and an axe. The gimlet is a long piece of iron wire with a flat point, fixed into a wooden handle consisting of two parts, the upper one of which is held in one hand, while the other is turned by a bow, whose string is twisted twice round it. The plane is small, but similar to that of Europe, excepting that it has a cross stick in the front, which serves as a handle for another workman, two being generally employed at one plane. As the comforts of a carpenter's bench are unknown, when a Hindoo wants to plane his work, he sits on the ground, with his partner opposite to him, steadying the timber with their toes, and both plane together. I have seen two of them working in this manner on a bit of wood a foot square, with a plane three inches long. Even the blacksmiths sit down to do their work; they dig a hole eighteen inches or two feet deep, in the centre of which they place the anvil, so that they can sit by it with their legs in the hole. A native of India does not get through so much work as an European; but the multitude of hands, and the consequent cheapness of labour, supply the place of the industry of Europe, and in most cases that of its machinery also. I saw the teak main-mast of the Minden, a weight of not less than twenty tons, lifted and moved a considerable distance by the koolis or porters. They carried it in slings fixed to bamboos, which they placed on their heads crosswise, with one arm over the bamboo, and the other on the shoulder of the man immediately before; in front of the whole marched one to guide and to clear the way, for, when they have once begun to move, the weight on the head prevents them from seeing what is before them.

In Bombay there are a good many Banyans, or travelling merchants, who come mostly from Guzerat, and roam about the country with muslins, cotton-cloth, and shawls, to sell. On opening one of their bales, I was surprised to find at least half of its contents of British manufacture, and such articles were much cheaper than those of equal fineness from Bengal and Madras. Excepting a particular kind of chintz made at Poonah, and painted with gold and silver, there are no fine cotton-cloths made on this side of the peninsula; yet still it seems strange, that cotton carried to England, manufactured, and returned to this country, should undersell the fabrics of India, where labour is so cheap. But I believe this is owing partly to the uncertainty and difficulty of carriage here, although the use of machinery at home must be the main cause. The shawls are brought here direct from Cashmeer, by the native merchants of that country, so that we sometimes get them cheap and beautiful. The Banyans ought to be Hindoos, though I have known Mussulmans adopt the name, with the profession; their distinguishing turban is so formed as to present the shape of a rhinoceros' horn in front, and it is generally red.

The *Borahs* are an inferior set of travelling-merchants. The inside of a *Borah's* box is like that of an English country shop, spelling-books, prayer-books, lavender-water, eau de luce, soap, tapes, scissars, knives, needles, and thread, make but a small part of the variety it contains. These people are Mussulmans, very poor, and reputed thieves. The profits on their trade must be very small; but the Banyans are often rich, and most of them keep a shop in the bazar, leaving one partner to attend it, while the other goes his rounds, attended by two or three koolis, with their loads on their heads.

It reminds one of the Arabian nights entertainments, to go through the bazar of an evening. The whole fronts of the shops are taken down and converted into benches, on which the goods are disposed, and each shop is lighted with at least two lamps. Here you see grain of every description heaped up in earthen jars; there, sweetmeats of all sorts and shapes, disposed in piles on benches, or hung in festoons about the top and sides of the shop, which is commonly lined with chintz or dyed cotton. Farther on, fruits and vegetables are laid out to the best advantage; then you come to the *paung*, or betel leaf, nut, and chunam, ready for chewing, or the separate materials; beyond are shops for perfumes, linens, oils, toys, brass, and earthen ware, all set out in order, and the owner sitting bolt upright in the middle of his sweetmeats or grain, waiting for custom. The shops of the *schroffs*, or bankers, are numerous in the bazar; you see the master sitting in the middle of his money table, surrounded by piles of copper and silver money, with scales for weighing the rupees and other coins presented for change. But it is the barber's shop that is always most crowded, being, particularly at night, the great resort for gossip and news; the barbers themselves seem to enjoy a prescriptive right to be lively, witty, and good story-tellers. I have seen some excellent buffoons among them, and a slap given to a bald new-shaven pate, in the proper part of a story, has set half a bazar in a roar. The barbers keep every body's holidays,—Hindoos, Jews, Mussulmans, Armenians, Portuguese, and English,—and reap a good harvest at each by their comic way of begging.

On first coming here, one would imagine that none of the people ever slept at night; for, besides that the coppersmiths and blacksmiths generally work all night, and sleep all day, on account of the heat, there are processions going about from sunset till sunrise, with *tom-toms*, (small drums,) kettle-drums, citarrs, vins, pipes, and a kind of large brazen trumpet, which requires two people to carry it, making altogether the most horrible din I ever heard. These processions, with the picturesque dresses of the natives, and their graceful attitudes, the torches carried by children, and the little double pipe blown by boys, whose wildness might make them pass for satyrs, put one strongly in mind of the ancient Bacchanals. It is usually on account of marriages that these nocturnal feasts are held; when they are in honour of a god they take place in the day, when the deity is carried on a litter in triumph, with banners before and behind, and priests carrying flowers, and milk and rice, while hardly any one joins the procession without an offering. All this looks very well at a distance, but when one comes near, one is shocked at the meanness and inelegance of the god, and at the filth and wretchedness of his votaries.

With one procession, however, I was much pleased; it took place a month ago in the breaking up of the monsoon, when the sea became open for navigation. It is called the coco-nut feast, and is, I believe, peculiar to this coast. About an hour before sunset, an immense concourse of people assembled on the esplanade, where booths were erected, with all kinds of commodities for sale. All the rich natives appeared in their carriages, and the display of pearls and jewels was astonishing. At sunset, one of the chief Bramins advanced towards the sea, and going out a little way upon a ledge of rock, he launched a gilt coco-nut, in token that the sea was now become navigable; immediately thousands of coco-nuts were seen swimming in the bay; for every priest and every master of a family was eager to make his offering. The evening closed as usual with music, dancing, and exhibitions of tumblers, jugglers, and tame snakes. The tumblers are usually from Hydrabad, the jugglers from Madras, and the exhibitions of snakes are common in every part of India. The agility and strength of the tumblers, particularly the women, surpassed every thing I ever saw; but the sight is rather curious than pleasant. The tame snakes are mostly cobra-capellas; at the sound of a small pipe, they rise on their tails, and spread their hoods, advance, retreat, hiss, and pretend to bite, at the word of command. The keepers wish it to be believed that they have the power of charming this animal, and preventing the bad effects of its bite; but I looked into the mouths of several, and found the teeth all gone, and the gums much lacerated. The method sometimes used to extract the teeth, is to throw a piece of red cloth to the snake, who bites it furiously; the keeper then takes him by the head, and holding his jaws forcibly together, tears out the cloth, and with it the teeth. The cobra-capella is from six to twelve feet long; it is held in great veneration by the natives, who call it a high caste snake, and do not willingly suffer it to be destroyed. There is a yearly feast and procession in honour of the snakes, when offerings of milk, rice, and sugar, are made to them, and money given to the priests, who, on these occasions, build rustic temples of bamboos and reeds in the fields.

November 20th.—A few days ago I was fortunate enough to make one of a party, assembled for the purpose of hearing from the Dustoor Moola Firoze an account of the actual state of the *Guebres* or *Parsees* in India. The Dustoor is the chief-priest of his sect in Bombay; he is a man of great learning; he passed six years in Persia, or, as he more classically calls it, Iraun, two of which were spent at Yezd, the only place where the Mussulman government tolerates a Guebre college. His manners are distinguished, and his person and address pleasing. He is a tall handsome man, of the middle age, with a lively and intelligent countenance; his dress is a long white muslin jamma, with a *cummerbund* or sash of beautiful shawl; another shawl was rolled round his high black cap, and a band of crimson velvet appeared between it and his brow.

The fragments of the ancient books of *Zoroaster* or *Zerdusht*, still extant, have been introduced in Europe by M. Anquetil, under the name of the *Zendavesta;* and there is a good deal of interesting matter concerning the establishment of *Pyrolatry* in Persia, in the Chevalier D'Ohsson's Tableau Historique de L'Orient, chiefly on the authority of the Shah Nameh of Firdousi *. But I do not know that there is any account of the present state of such of the Guebres as are settled in India; and as these people form the richest class of inhabitants in Bombay, I have taken some pains to collect what information I could concerning them, both from Moola Firoze and other individuals of the nation.

It appears that there have been two legislators of the name of Zoroaster, one of whom lived in times of such remote antiquity, that no dependence can be placed on the traditions concerning him. The last flourished as late as the reign of Darius the son of Cambyses. He appears to have reformed the religion of his country, which there is reason to think was till that time the same with that of India, to have built the first fine temples, and to have written the books of Guebre laws, of which only some fragments remain †.

* For an account of the Shah Nameh, see Appendix.

† See a curious traditional account of *Zerdusht* in Herbert's Travels, pp. 48. to 54. This amusing traveller gives an account of the Parsees of Guzerat, as he found them when he accompanied Sir Robert Shirly on his last embassy to Persia.

The Parsees acknowledge a good principle under the name of Hormuzd, and an evil principle under that of Ahrimane. Subordinate to Hormuzd, the *ferishta*, or angels, are charged with the creation and preservation of the material world. The sun, the moon, and the stars, the years, the months, and the days, have each their presiding angel; angels attend on every human soul, and an angel receives it when it leaves the body. *Myrh*, or *Mithra*, is the ferishta to whom this important charge is assigned, as well as that of judging the dead; he is also the guardian of the sun, and presides over the sixth month, and the sixth day of the month. The good ferishta have corresponding evil genii, who endeavour to counteract them in all their functions; they particularly encourage witchcraft, and willingly hold converse with enchanters of both sexes, sometimes revealing truly the secrets of futurity for malicious purposes. As in other countries, the old, the ugly, and the miserable, are stigmatized as witches, and the Indian Bramins are regarded by the Guebres as powerful magicians.

Fire is the chief object of external worship among the Parsees. In each *atsh-khaneh*, or fire-house, there are two fires, one of which it is lawful for the vulgar to behold, but the other, *atsh-baharam*, is kept in the most secret and holy part of the temple, and is approached only by the chief dustoor; it must not be visited by the light of the sun, and the chimneys for carrying off the smoke are so constructed as to exclude his rays. The atsh-baharam must be composed of five different kinds of fire, among which I was surprised to hear the dustoor mention that of a funeral pile, as the Guebres expose their dead; but he told me that it was formerly lawful to return the body to any of the four elements; that is, to bury it in the earth or in the water, to burn, or to expose it, but that the latter only is now practised; consequently, if the atsh-baharam goes out, they must travel to such nations as burn their dead, to procure the necessary ingredient to rekindle it. When the last atsh-khaneh was built in Bombay, a portion of the sacred fire was brought from the altar at Yezd, in a golden censer, by land, that it might not be exposed to the perils of the sea.

The sun and the sea partake with fire in the adoration of the Guebres. Their prayers called *zemzemé*, are repeated in a low murmuring tone, with the face turned towards the rising or the setting sun, and obeisance is made to the sea and to the full moon. The Parsee year is divided into twelve lunar months, with intercalary days, but there is no division of time into weeks. The festivals are the *nowroze*, or day of the new year, and six following days; the first of every month; and the day on which the name of the day and that of the month agree, when the same ferishta presides over both.

A Parsee marries but one wife, excepting when he has no children; then, with the consent of the first, he may take a second. An adopted child inherits equally with legitimate children, but, if there be none, before all other relations. The death of a father is observed as an annual festival. The body must not touch wood after death; it is accordingly laid upon an iron bier, to be conveyed to the repository for the dead, where it is left exposed to the air till it is consumed. In Bombay these repositories are square inclosures, surrounded by high walls; the vulgar Parsees superstitiously watch the corpse, to see which eye is first devoured by the birds, and thence augur the happiness or misery of the soul.

The sacred books are in the Zend and Pehlavi languages, both ancient dialects of Persia. The fragments of these which escaped during the troubles that followed the Mahomedan conquest of Persia, are all that the Guebres have to direct either their practice or their faith; and where these are found insufficient, the dustoors supply rules from their own judgment. The chief doctrines of the remaining books respect future rewards and punishments, injunctions to honour parents, and to marry early, that the chain of being be not interrupted, and prohibitions of murder, theft, and adultery.

When the Guebres were driven from their own country by the Mussulmans *, a considerable body of them resolved to seek a new land, and accordingly put to sea, where they suffered great hardships. After attempting to settle in various places, they at length reached Sunjum in Guzerat, and sent their chief dustoor, Abah, on shore, to ask an asylum. This was granted by the Rajah on certain conditions, and a treaty to the following effect was drawn up: The Guebres shall have a place allotted to them for the performance of their religious and burial rites; they shall have lands for the maintenance of themselves and their families; they shall conform to the Hindoo customs with regard to marriages, and in their dress; they shall not carry arms; they

* The conquest of the kingdom of Fars, or Persia, took place in the seventh century, when Yezdegerd, the last king of the dynasty of Sassan, was overcome by the Calif Omar, and forced to take refuge in the mountains of Khorassan, where, after maintaining himself for some time, he died, A. D. 652. A. H. 32. and in the 21st year of the Yedegerdian æra. His grand-daughter became the wife of the Mussulman ruler of Persia, who thus claimed the right of inheritance, as well as that of conquest, over the kingdom.

shall speak the language of Guzerat, that they may become as one people with the original inhabitants; and they shall abstain from killing and eating the cow. To these conditions the Parsees have scrupulously adhered, and they have always been faithful to their protectors.

The Parsees in British India enjoy every privilege, civil and religious. They are governed by their own *panchait*, or village council. The word panchait literally means a council of five, but that of the Guebres in Bombay consists of thirteen of the principal merchants of the sect; these were chosen originally by the people, confirmed by the government, and have continued hereditary. This little council decides all questions of property, subject, however, to an appeal to the recorder's court; but an appeal seldom happens, as the panchaït is jealous of its authority, and is consequently cautious in its decisions. It superintends all marriages and adoptions, and inquires into the state of every individual of the community; its members would think themselves disgraced if any Parsee were to receive assistance from a person of a different faith; accordingly, as soon as the children of a poor man are old enough to marry, which, in conformity to the Hindoo custom, is at five or six years of age, the chief merchants subscribe a sufficient sum to portion the child; in cases of sickness, they support the individual or the family, and maintain all the widows and fatherless.

The panchaït consists both of dustoors and laymen; all religious ceremonies and festivals come under its cognizance, together with the care of the temples, the adjusting the almanack, and the subsistence and life of the dogs. I could not learn with certainty the origin of the extreme veneration of the Parsees for this animal; every morning the rich merchants employ koolis to go round the streets with baskets of provision for the wild dogs; and, when a Parsee is dying, he must have a dog in his chamber to fix his closing eyes upon. Some believe that the dog guards the soul, at the moment of its separation from the body, from the evil spirits; others say that the veneration for the dogs is peculiar to the Indian Guebres, and that it arose from their having been saved from shipwreck in their emigration to India, by the barking of the dogs announcing their approach to the land in a dark night.

The Parsees use some solemnities when they name their children, which is done at five or six months old; when the muslin shirt is put on the first time, a sacred fire is lighted, prayers are repeated, and the name is given. Since their intercourse with Europeans, they persist in calling this ceremony christening, because it is performed when the first or proper name is given; the second name is a patronymic; thus, *Norozejee Jumsheedjee*, is Norozejee the son of Jumsheedjee.

The Parsees are the richest individuals on this side of India, and most of the great merchants are partners in British commercial houses. They have generally two or three fine houses, besides those they let to the English; they keep a number of carriages and horses, which they lend willingly, not only to Europeans, but to their own poor relations, whom they always support. They often give dinners to the English gentlemen, and drink a great deal of wine, particularly Madeira. The Guebre women enjoy more freedom than other oriental females, but they have not yet thought of cultivating their minds. Perhaps this is owing in great measure to the early marriages which, in compliance with the Hindoo customs, they contract. By becoming the property of their husbands in their infancy, they never think of acquiring a further share of their affection, and, with the hope of pleasing, one great incitement to mental improvement is cut off.

Some days ago, we all spent an evening with the family of Pestenjee Bomanjee, for they admit men as well as women to the ladies' apartments. The women were fair and handsome, with pleasing manners; they were loaded with ornaments, particularly the largest and finest pearls I ever saw. Pestengee's grandson, a child of seven years old, with his little wife, two years younger, appeared with strings of pearls as large as hazel-nuts, besides five or six long rows of the size of peas, and beautifully regular, given to them on their marriage, which happened a few months ago, on a lucky day and in a lucky month; for the Parsees, like the Hindoos, regulate all their actions by the motions and configurations of the stars, or rather by the interpretations of the astrologers. It is not uncommon for a rich man to spend a lack of rupees, (about twelve thousand five hundred pounds sterling) at the marriage of a child. Streets both carpeted and canopied with cotton cloth, confectionary and fruit scattered among the populace, feasting for several days for all ranks of people, processions and fire-works all night, and whole bazars illuminated, besides gifts to relations and dependents, account for the immense sums spent on these occasions. The little bride and bridegroom, borne on an ornamented palankeen, covered with jewels and flowers, preceded by banners and musical instruments, and followed by crowds of people, seem like little victims going to sacrifice, at least I cannot help considering them in that light.

The grandfather of Pestengee was Lowjee, who came from Guzerat to work in the dock-yard as a day-labourer; but having genius and perseverance, he made himself master of the art of ship-building, and was employed by the Company as master-builder. He has transmitted his talents with his place to his grandson Jumsheedjee, who is now at the head of the dock-yard, where I visited him, and was conducted by him all over the Minden, the first line of battle ship he ever built, with the pride of a parent exhibiting a favourite child. It was singular enough at first to see all the ship-wrights in white muslin dresses, caulking the ship with cotton instead of oakum. All the workmen in the yard are Parsees, and the greater number come from Guzerat, where they leave their families, and come to Bombay for a few months or years, saving their wages carefully, and mostly subsisting on what they earn by chance-work, till they have amassed a sufficient sum to go home and set up a trade for themselves. Jumsheedjee is a clever workman, but his son Norozejee has more science, and I am told that his draughts have very great merit. This young man testifies the greatest desire to visit the great English yards, but his father cannot spare him from Bombay. The whole family, including Pestengee and Hormuzdjee, the brothers of Jumsheedjee, speak and write English so well, that if I did not see their dark faces and foreign dress, or read their unusual names at the end of a letter, I should never guess that they were not Englishmen.

The Parsees are in general a handsome large people, but they have a more vulgar air than the other natives; they are extremely active and enterprising, and are liberal in their opinions, and less bigotted to their own customs, manners, and dress, than most nations. Of their hospitality and charitable dispositions, the following is an instance. During the famine that desolated India in the years 1805 and 1806, the Parsee merchant Ardeseer Dadee, fed five thousand poor persons for three months at his own expense, besides other liberalities to the starving people. The Parsees are the chief landholders in Bombay. Almost all the houses and gardens inhabited by the Europeans are their property; and Pestengee told me that he received not less than L. 15,000 a-year in rents, and that his brother received nearly as much.

November 24.—At length we have accomplished a visit to Elephanta and its wonderful excavations; but as a description of these, and the sculpture that adorns them, would not be intelligible without at least a slight previous acquaintance with the principal gods of Hindostan, I shall set down a brief account of them before I describe the cavern.

The ancient system of religion in India, seems to have been far from admitting the multitude of persons now worshipped *.

* "It is universally known that the Hindoos are divided into various sects, but their characteristic differences are not perhaps so generally understood. Five great sects exclusively worship a single deity; one recognizes the five divinities which are adored by the other sects respectively; but the followers of this comprehensive scheme mostly select one object of daily devotion, and pay adoration to the other deities on particular occasions. Even they deny the charge of polytheism, and repel the imputation of idolatry; they justify the practice of adoring the images of celestial spirits, by arguments similar to those which have been elsewhere employed in support of image worship. If the doctrines of the Vedas, and even those of the Puranas, be closely examined, the Hindoo theology will be found *consistent monotheism,* though it contains the seeds of polytheism and idolatry."

COLEBROOK, Note on 9th Art. Vol. 7. As. Res.

The five great sects are; Saivas, adoring Siva or Maha Deo; the Vaisnavas, adoring Vishnu; the Sauras, Surya or the sun; the Ganepatyas or Gosseins, Gundputti or Ganesa; and the Sactis, Bawanee or Parvati. The Bhagavates ought to recognize

Brehm was the only one, the eternal, the almighty. His energy exerted, divided, and personified, became, Brahma to create, Vishnu to preserve, and Siva to destroy; thus the three greatest and most striking operations of nature, became the offices of peculiar gods. But as things once created are never wholly destroyed, and their elements appear again in other forms, Siva the destroyer is also the god of reproduction, and the creating power of Brahma lies dormant till it shall be exerted in a new formation of the world. Accordingly his temples are fallen into decay, and I believe that he is seldom or never now adored. Each of these three gods is provided with a *sacti* or wife, who partakes of the nature and offices of her husband, and is considered as his active power or energy. Having advanced so far towards polytheism, it was natural to multiply the gods, as the operations of nature and the wants of mankind came to be observed and felt; and while the legislators and priests might adore but one god in spirit and in truth, his personified attributes would indubitably be worshipped as independent deities by the vulgar.

In the common mythological accounts of the creation, Vishnu is fabled to have slept on the serpent Annanta or eternity, floating on the face of the milky ocean. When the work of creation was to be performed, Brahma sprang from a lotus growing on the navel of Vishnu, and produced the elements, formed the world, and gave birth to the human race. From different parts of his body he produced the Bramins or priests, the Xetries or warriors, the Vaisyas or merchants, and the Soodras or hus-

all these deities as subordinate to the Supreme Being, or rather as his attributes, but the greater part of them are real polytheists. There is an inconsiderable sect of gymnosophists, called Lingis, who adore Siva exclusively.

bandmen; which four original castes, by intermarriages, and by the adoption of different trades, have multiplied exceedingly. Brahma is often represented with four faces, when he is called *Choturmooki*; he is sometimes seen studying the vedas, which he holds in one hand, while the other three are employed holding his beads * and sacrificial utensils; he generally sits on a lotus.

The wife of Brahma is Seraswati, also called Brahmanee; she is the goddess of arts and eloquence, and is often invoked with Ganesa at the beginning of books. As the patroness of music, she is sometimes represented with a vin † in her hand. Menu, and ten other lawgivers, are the children of Brahma and Seraswati; from Menu and his wife the earth was peopled, and Menu gave to his descendants excellent laws, but they did not abide by them; therefore other Menus have at different times been born, to recall mankind to the belief and practice of their ancestors. Among the animal creation, the goose, the emblem of wisdom, is sacred to Seraswati, who, as well as Brahma, is often seen riding on it, when it is called their vahan or vehicle.

Siva is worshipped more generally than any of the other deities. His principal names are, *Doorghatti*, *Isa*, *Iswara*, *Hurr*, *Rudra*, and *Maha Deo*. Under the last name, all his temples on this side of India are dedicated to him as the god of reproduction. As Rudra he is terrible, and delights in sanguinary sacrifices, particularly the *aswa-medha* or horse sacrifice, and the *nara-medha*, or human sacrifice.

* Both the Hindoos and Mussulmen use strings of beads for the purpose of counting their prayers.

† *Vin*, a musical instrument played like the guitar; it consists of a long board, on which the strings of iron wire are placed, with a hollow gourd at each end, as a sounding-board.

The wife of Siva is *Parvati*, or the mountain-born. Her celestial name is *Doorga* or active virtue; as *Bhawani*, she is female nature on earth; and as *Kali*, she is an infernal goddess, delighting in human sacrifice, and, like Rudra, wearing a chaplet of skulls round her neck. The residence of Siva and Parvati is Kaylassa; their constant attendant is the bull *Nundi*, who is usually placed at the gates or in the courts of their temples. In the character of Doorga, Parvati is always attended by a lion.

Kartikeya, or *Swammy-kartic*, and *Ganesa*, are the children of Siva and Parvati. Kartikeya is the god of war, and leader of the celestial armies; he is mounted on a peacock. He has six faces, and is fabled to have been nursed by the six *Kritikas*, or stars of the Pleïades, who are the wives of the *Rooshis*, or stars of the constellation of the Great Bear. *Ganesa* is the god of wisdom; he is often the god of fortune, and presides over the limits of fields. He is represented very fat, with the head of an elephant, having sometimes two and sometimes four faces. He holds in his hands a cup containing round cakes, which he appears to be eating, and the ankasa, or hook used by the drivers of elephants, which has been taken for a key, and supposed to confirm the identity of this god with Janus. Ganesa is invoked the first in all sacrifices, and all writings begin with his name. He is always attended by a rat, the emblem of forethought.

Vishnu, the preserving deity, exclusive of his names in his several *awatars*, is *Narayun*, or moving on the ocean, *Shreedher*, *Govinda*, and *Hari*. His wife is *Luckshemi*, the goddess of fortune, called also Kamala, or the lotus-born, having sprung on a lotus from the ocean. She is the goddess of beauty, and presides over marriage. Her son Camdeo is the god of beauty and of love. It is related in the Ramayuna, that Camdeo or Kundurpa, having presumed to wound Siva, while with uplifted arm he was engaged in sacred austerities, the incensed god consumed his body with lightning from his eyes. Hence Camdeo is called *Ununga*, bodyless, and he is the only person in the Hindoo mythology who is ever said to be immaterial. He is sometimes called *Muddun*, and rides on a fish, with a banner in his hand.

Vishnu is often seen riding on the shoulders of Garuda, a youth with the wings and beak of a hawk; but he is more frequently represented reposing on the great many-headed serpent of eternity, floating on the milky ocean; in which case Luckshemi is generally sitting at his feet. The Hindoos believe that the four yougs * must revolve seventy-two times in every kalpa, (creation or formation), at the end of which all things are absorbed into the Deity, and that, in the interval of another creation, he reposeth himself on the serpent Shesha (duration), who is called Ananta (endless) †. Many of the offices of Vishnu are common both to Brahma and to Siva; and the names of all three are frequently used for the sun, for fire, and for water. Each deity has weapons peculiar to himself; those which always distinguish Vishnu are the *chakra* or discus, and the *chank* or wreathed shell, on which the note of victory is sounded. The paradise of Vishnu is Vaikontha; he is often painted of a dark blue colour, on which account he is called Nielkont.

The awatars of Vishnu, by which are meant his descents upon earth, are usually counted ten, though some writers make them

* The first, or the Kruty-youg; it lasts 17 lacks and 25,000 years. The second, or Treta-youg, 12 lacks and 296,000 years. The third, or Dwapar-youg, lasts 8 lacks and 64,000 years: And the 4th, or Kali-youg, 4 lacks and 32,000 years. In this we now live. PUNDIT BAPOOGEE.

† See Notes to the Heetopadesa.

much more numerous. The first is the Mutchee or fish awatar, when, in the form of a huge fish, he conducted and preserved the boat of Styavrata the 7th menu, while the earth was deluged in consequence of the loss of the vedas, and the subsequent wickedness of mankind. The holy books had been stolen by Hyagriva, king of the demons; Vishnu undertook to recover them; and, after a severe combat with Hyagriva, he destroyed him, restored the sacred books, and caused the waters to subside. The second awatar is Koorma, or the tortoise. In order to recover some of the advantages lost to mankind by the deluge, Vishnu became a tortoise, and sustained on his back the mountain Meru, while the gods and genii churned with it the milky ocean, and produced seven precious things, among which were, the moon, a physician, a horse, a woman, an elephant, and *Amrita*, or the water of life, which was drank by the immortals. The third awatar is Varaha, or the boar. *Prit'hivi*, the earth, having been overcome by the genius of the waters, Vishnu, in the shape of a man, with the head of a hog, descended and supported her on his tusk, while he subdued the waters and restored her. In the fourth awatar, Vishnu, in the form of a monstrous man, with a lion's head, sprang from a pillar to destroy an impious king who was on the point of murdering his own son. He is called Narasinha, or lion-headed. Vishnu, in his fifth descent, is called Vamuna, or the Brahmin dwarf. Beli having, by his meritorious austerities, obtained the sovereignty of the world, neglected to worship the gods; the Dewtahs, alarmed lest he should deprive them of their celestial habitations, entreated protection from Vishnu, who descended in the form of a Bramin dwarf, and having obtained from Beli a promise, confirmed by an irrevocable oath, to grant whatever he should ask, he demanded as much space as he could compass in three steps. The boon being granted, his form dilated to its divine dimensions; the eight celestial weapons appeared in the eight hands of the god, whose first step compassed the earth, his second the ocean, and his third heaven, leaving only Patala or hell to Beli. Vamuna is sometimes called *Tri-vikrum*, or three-stepper. In the sixth awatar, Vishnu, as Parashu Rama, the son of the Bramin Jemadagni, is fabled to have destroyed all the males of the Xetrie or fighting caste, on account of the wickedness of their chief Sahasrarjum, who oppressed the Bramins, particularly Jemadagni. The seventh descent of Vishnu is sung in the epic poem of Valmiki, called the Ramayuna, from Rama the divine hero, the son of Dusharuthra, king of *Uyodhya* or Oude, who led a life of adventure in the woods and forests of India, attended by his brother Lakshmana, and by his faithful friend Hanuman the divine monkey, the son of Pavana, god of the wind. Sita, the wife of Rama, having been stolen by Rawana the ten-headed tyrant of *Lanka* (Ceylon), Hanuman discovered the place of her concealment, and with the assistance of Soogreeva and other divine baboons, he built the bridge of Rama (Adam's bridge,) from the continent of India to Ceylon, to facilitate the passage of Rama and his army to that island, where he destroyed the tyrant and recovered Sita.

Krishna, the person in whom Vishnu was incarnate in his eighth awatar, is said to have been born of the sister of a tyrant, who, to secure the death of his nephew, caused all the young children in his dominions to be put to death; but, in the mean time, the young Krishna was concealed and brought up among some herdsmen, whence he is considered as the peculiar patron of herds, and is often represented as attended by nine Gopia or dairy-women. He is the god of poetry and music, of wrestlers and of boxers. The adventures of Krishna, and the wars in which he was engaged, are described in the Bhagavat. The ninth awatar is Bhûd, who reformed the rules of the vedas, and forbid the destroying animal life. The tenth awatar, called Kalkee, is to come. He will be a warrior on a white horse; in his days the world shall be at peace, all enmity shall be destroyed, and men shall have but one faith.

Of the religious sects worshipping Vishnu, the Vaishnavas adore him alone, as comprising in his person the greatest number of the attributes of the deity. The Goclasthas and the Ramanuj are in fact worshippers of deified heroes; the first pay respect to Vishnu in the awatar of Gocal or Krishna, and the second in that of Rama Chandra.

Besides the great deities above-mentioned, there are multitudes of inferior divine persons, over whom Indra, the thousand-eyed lord of the dewtahs presides. He dwells with his wife Indranee in the forest Nundana, and with her is often seen mounted on an elephant with three trunks. He presides over delusions. Agni, the god of fire, is represented with two faces and three legs, riding on a ram. He is said to have married the goddess Gunga (Ganges,) the sister of Parvati. Gunga is fabled to have rested on the head of Siva, or that of Vishnu, in her descent from heaven, and to have flowed thence in three streams, called *triveni*, or three locks, and running to the sea, to have filled up its bason, which, although dug before that time, was empty. Her union with Agni produced the metals. The range of mountains among which the Ganges takes its rise, abounds with mines; hence the mythological union of the deities of heat and of water is fabled to have produced the metals. Surya, the god of the sun, is drawn in a chariot by a many-headed horse; he represents truth, and has a numerous sect of worshippers called Sauras. Chandra, the moon, is drawn in a car by an antelope; the twenty-seven lunar stations, called Nukshutras, into which the Hindoos divide the heavens, are considered as his wives.

Viswakarman is the artificer of the gods; Koovera is the god of riches, and resides in the forest of Chitra-ruthra; and Pavana is the god of the wind. Eight guardians preside over the eight quarters of the world; and all nature is crowded with deities.

In making this slight sketch of the Hindoo mythology, I have forborne to point out the striking similarity of many of the deities to those of Greece and Rome, as it is too obvious to escape your attention. A remarkable proof of their identity with the gods of Egypt occurred in 1801, when the sepoy regiments who had been sent into that country, fell down before the gods in the temple of Tentyra, and claimed them as those of their own belief. The coarseness and inelegance of the Hindoo polytheism, will certainly disgust many accustomed to the graceful mythology of ancient Europe; but it is not incurious, nor perhaps useless, to examine the various systems of religion which the feelings natural to the mind of man have produced,—to observe how they have been modified by climate or other circumstances,—and to trace, "under all these "various disguises, the workings of the same common nature; "and in the superstitions of *India*, no less than in the lofty visions of Plato, to recognize the existence of those moral ties "which unite the heart of man to the Author of his being*." For my own part, living among the people, and daily beholding the prostrate worshipper, the temple, the altar, and the offering, I take an interest in them which makes up for their want of poe-

* Stewart's Elements of the Philosophy of the Human Mind.

tical beauty. Nor can I look with indifference upon a system, however barbarous and superstitious, which has so strong a hold of the minds of its votaries, and which can bring them to despise death and torture in their most dreadful forms.

But to return to my journal. We got into our boat at Mazagong a little before sunrise, and had the pleasure of marking the gradual increase of day as it broke over the Mahratta mountains. First the woody tops of Caranja and Elephanta became illuminated, then Bombay, with its forts and villages stretching along the north of the bay, while the bases of the rocky islands to the south, slowly became distinguishable from the reflecting waves. After an hour's row, during which we passed Butcher's Island, called by the natives Deva Devi, or holy island, we arrived at Elephanta, a mountain isle with a double top, wooded to the summit. Opposite to the landing-place is the colossal stone elephant, from which the Portuguese named the place, which is now cracked and mutilated, as tradition says, by the Portuguese; it must have been carved out of the rock on which it stands, for it appears too large to have been carried to its present situation. After passing a village which, as well as the whole island, the natives call Gharipoori, we ascended the hill through romantic passes, sometimes overshadowed with wood, sometimes walled by rocks, till we arrived at the cave. We came upon it unexpectedly, and I confess that I never felt such a sensation of astonishment as when the cavern opened upon me. At first it appeared all darkness, while on the hill above, below, and around, shrubs and flowers of the most brilliant hues were waving in the full sunshine. As I entered, my sight became gradually more distinct, and I was able to consider the wonderful chamber in which I stood. The entrance is fifty-five feet wide, its height is eigh-

teen, and its length about equal with its width. It is supported by massy pillars carved in the solid rock; the capital of these resembles a compressed cushion bound with a fillet; the abacus is like a bunch of reeds supporting a beam, six of which run across the whole cave; below the capital the column may be compared to a fluted bell resting on a plain octagonal member placed on a die, on each corner of which sits Hanuman, Ganesa, or some of the other inferior gods. The sides of the cavern are sculptured in compartments representing the persons of the mythology; but the end of the cavern opposite to the entrance is the most remarkable. In the centre is a gigantic trimurti, or three-formed god. Brahma the creator is in the middle, with a placid countenance; his cap is adorned with jewels. Vishnu, the preserving deity, is represented as very beautiful; his face is full of benevolence, his hand holds a lotus, the same sacred flower is placed in his cap, with the triveni or triple-plaited lock, signifying the rivers Gunga (Ganges), Yamuna (Jumna), and Seraswati, and other ornaments referring to his attributes. Siva frowns, his nose is aquiline, and his mouth half open; in his hand is his destructive emblem, the cobra-capella, and on his cap, among other symbols, a human skull and a new-born infant mark his double character of destroyer and reproducer. These faces are all beautiful but for the under lips, which are remarkably thick. The length from the chin to the crown of the head is six feet, the caps are about three feet more. No part of the bust is mutilated but the two hands in front, which are quite destroyed. Concealed steps behind Siva's hand lead to a convenient ledge or bench behind the cap of the bust, where a Bramin might have hidden himself for any purpose of priestly imposition. On each side of the trimurti is a pilaster, the front of which is filled up by a figure fourteen feet high, leaning on a dwarf; these are much defaced. To the right is a large square compartment, hollowed a little, carved into a great variety of figures, the largest of which is sixteen feet high, representing the double figure of Siva and Parvati, called Viraj or Ardha Nari, half male half female, the right side of which is Siva and the left his wife; it is four-handed; the two lower hands, one of which appears to have rested on the *Nundi*, are broken; the upper right hand has a cobra-capella, and the left a shield. On the right of the Viraj is Brama, four-faced, sitting on a lotus; and on the left is Vishnu on the shoulders of Garuda. Near Brahma are Indra and Indranee on their elephant, and below is a female figure holding a chamara or chowree *. The upper part of the compartment is filled with small figures in attitudes of adoration.

On the other side of the trimurti is a compartment answering to that I have just described; the principal figure I take to be Siva; at his left hand stands Parvati, on whose shoulder he leans; between them is a dwarf, on whose head is one of Siva's hands, and near Parvati is another. Over Siva's shoulder hangs the zenaar, and he holds the cobra-capella in one of his four hands. He is surrounded by the same figures which fill up the compartment of the Viraj; his own height (which we measured by a plumb-line dropped from his head,) is fourteen feet, and that of Parvati is ten. All these figures are in alto-relievo, as are those of the other sides of the cavern, the most remarkable of which is one of Siva in his vindictive character; he is eight-handed,

* The chamara is a whisk to keep off flies, made either of a cow's tail or peacock's feathers, or ivory shavings, set in a handle two feet long. They are always carried behind persons of rank.

with a chaplet of skulls round his neck, and appears in the act of performing the human sacrifice.

On the right hand, as you enter the cave, is a square apartment with four doors, supported by eight colossal figures; it contains a gigantic symbol of Maha Deo, and is cut out of the rock like the rest of the cave. There is a similar chamber in a smaller and more secret cavern, to which there is access from the corner next to the Viraj; the covering of the passage has fallen in, but, on climbing over the rubbish, we found ourselves in a little area which has no outlet, and is lighted from above, the whole thickness of the hill being cut through; the cavern to which it belongs contains nothing but the square chamber of Maha Deo, and a bath at each end, one of which is decorated with rich sculpture.

When we had tired ourselves with examining the various wonders of the cavern of Elephanta, I sat down to make a sketch of the great compartments opposite to the entrance, and on our return to Bombay, comparing the drawing with those in Niebuhr, we were satisfied that its resemblance to the original is the most correct*. I am sorry to observe, that the pillars and sculptures of the cave are defaced in every part, by having the names of most who visit them either carved or daubed with black chalk upon them; and the intemperate zeal of the Portuguese, who made war upon the gods and temples, as well as upon the armies of India, added to the havock of time, has reduced this stupendous monument of idolatry to a state of ruin. Fragments of statues strew the floor;

* From this sketch the annexed plate is copied. The trimurti is imperfect; that having been separately drawn by a friend, from whom I have not been able to procure a correct copy.

columns, deprived of their bases, are suspended from the parent roof, and others without capitals, and sometimes split in two, threaten to leave the massy hill that covers them without support.

The temple of Elephanta, and other equally wonderful caverns in the neighbourhood, must have been the works of a people far advanced in the arts of civilized life, and possessed of wealth and power; but these were lodged in the hands of a crafty priesthood, who kept science, affluence, and honour for their own fraternity, and, possessed of better ideas, preached a miserable and degrading superstition to the multitude. It would be curious to follow out the advancement and fall of the arts which produced such monuments; but not a trace of their history remains, and we are left to seek it in the natural progress of a people subtle and ingenious, but depressed by superstition, and the utter impossibility of rising individually, by any virtues or any talents, to a higher rank in society than that occupied by their forefathers.

The local histories * of the Braminical establishments, which could have thrown light on these and other curious subjects, have long been destroyed. Many of them perished during the contentions between the followers of Siva and those of Vishnu, prior to the Mahomedan conquest of India, and probably many more

* *Stala Puranas* are literally the church books; they are registers belonging to the temples, in which are marked all benefactors, and their donations to the sacred establishments, and in general the dates of such donations. But even these documents are filled with fables. For instance, a pious prince who would build a temple, is usually directed to the exact spot by an apparition or a dream; the idols he sets up are discovered to him in the same miraculous manner, and most of these are heaven-descended for the occasion!

when the Hindoo temples were pillaged by those fierce conquerors.

It is said that there are some other caves on the island of Elephanta, but I have never met with any one who had explored them, and I conclude that they are insignificant. We remained all day in the great temple, enjoying its coolness, while the burning tropical sun shone most fiercely above; but as soon as the day began to close we left it, to the great regret of the hamauls who had accompanied us, and who, after cooking and eating in one corner of the cave, had employed themselves in pouring water over the gods, and in sprinkling them with flowers. The little village of Gharipoori has a few rice fields, and its inhabitants rear poultry and mutton. The island abounds with springs of excellent water, and the luxuriant growth of the wood gives it a more fertile appearance than any part of Bombay; nevertheless it is almost a desert.

We intended to have visited Butcher's Island on our way home, but we had stayed too long in the cave, and were obliged to pass its low green plain and tufts of trees, just as the setting sun threw his last beams across the bay.

Panwell, Dec. 14*th* 1809.—I am writing in a tent pitched in the rice fields of Panwell, a little Mahratta village on the coast. Taking advantage of the cool season, we have joined a small party on a tour to Poonah, the Mahratta capital. Our company consists of one lady, two gentlemen, and three children, besides ourselves, but our attendants are near two hundred; we are obliged to carry tents, furniture, cooking utensils, and food, so that our train cannot consist of fewer persons. Besides, we must have koolis to carry our baggage, lascars to attend to and pitch our tents, servants to dress our food, others to take care of the horses and the beasts of burthen, and hamauls for our palankeens. Having sent on the baggage and servants the preceding day, we embarked at the bunder in the fort of Bombay, and after a three hours sail we reached Panwell, situated two miles inland, on a branch of the sea, the entrance to which is marked rather than defended by the little ruinous fort of Bellapoor. This fort was built in 1682 by the Mahratta Rajah Sambagee, to protect the Corlahs, or low districts in this neighbourhood, from the irruptions of the Siddees, then in the service of the Mogul, and who used to land from their numerous vessels, and carry off or burn the rice, in which the Corlahs were then more fertile than any of the Mahratta provinces.

On our arrival here, we found our tents pitched in some dry *paddy* (rice) fields, by the side of a large tank surrounded by Mango trees. On one side is a *Pirs Kubber*, or Mahomedan saint's tomb, of a beautiful form, with an arcade, the arches of which are like the Gothic, with cinquefoil heads; the cell within contains the tomb, covered with a piece of brocade; over it is a canopy, from which a number of lamps and ostrich eggs are suspended.

The village is well peopled, its inhabitants look comfortable, and the fields cultivated. Here is a large pagoda by a tank, nearly a mile in circumference, on the water of which float multitudes of the beautiful red lotus; the flower is larger than that of the white water-lily, and is the most lovely of the nymphæas that I have seen. The natives of Panwell have a more martial air than those of Bombay. In the shops, every artizan has his sword and spear by him while he works, and the cultivators plough with their arms girded on. At present their weapons are of more use to defend them against the wild beasts than against any human enemy, but a few years ago the case was otherwise.

Dec. 16*th.* *Compowli.*—This village is two stages from Panwell; the first, to Chowk, we travelled last night, but reached our tents too late to write. We passed through a very beautiful country, among hills that form the outskirts of the Ghauts *. Rich valleys, now wide now narrow, closed in by amphitheatres of hills, some wooded up to the top, and others exposing their weather-stained rocky summits to the skies, are here and there crossed by streams, that though now scarcely more than rills, bear evidence that they were mighty torrents during the monsoon. Upon the bank of one of these, we encamped under the shade of wide-spreading banian trees, opposite to the little bazar of Chowk. Immediately facing us, a troop of Brinjarees had taken up their residence for the night. These people travel from one end of India to the other, carrying salt, grain, and asafœtida, almost as necessary to the natives as salt. They are never molested by any army. I have seen at least five hundred bullocks belonging to one troop. You can imagine nothing more picturesque than our station: the Brinjarees fires were reflected in the stream between us; and our own hamauls, in about a dozen different parties, were cooking their food along the bank, while at a little distance some of our people were keeping up a blaze with straw, to keep the flies from the horses, the bright light from which falling on our tents illuminated them, while the under

* A ghaut means a pass; and though it literally applies only to the accessible passes through the mountains, the name is given to the range of mountains that reach from Cape Comorin nearly to Guzerat, along the west coast of India.

branches of the trees remaining in shadow, formed a striking and beautiful contrast. When we went to rest, our dining tent was struck, that it might go on before, in order to be ready for breakfast at the next stage, where we now are.

When we left Chowk at day-break this morning, the thermometer was at sixty-eight in my palankeen, but before we arrived at Compowli it had risen more than twenty-two degrees. We were nearly four hours on the road, although the distance is not more than twelve miles; the way lies through the same kind of country as that between Chowk and Panwell, only that it is more picturesque and wild, and reminded me of Scotish Highland scenery. Our tents are pitched in a *tope* or grove of mango trees, by the side of a spacious tank, overhung by a fine old banian tree. Behind us is a hill wooded to the top; immediately opposite is a beautiful little pagoda, which, as well as the tank, was built by Nana Furnavese, the late Mahratta minister, though himself a Pundit, and therefore, in all probability, a secret unbeliever. But in India, where the long continued droughts render water an object of such importance, he who builds a tank is a benefactor to his country; and unless it be rendered sacred by being attached to a pagoda, the first army that passes would in all probability break down its dikes, and thus cause the destruction of men and cattle by drought and famine, for the fields produce no crops without constant irrigation.

At the back of Nana's pagoda the ghaut rises perpendicularly, and seems almost to overhang it; and a few coco-nuts and plantains in its garden, make an agreeable variety with the tufted foliage of the mountain-forest. The temple is dedicated to Maha Deo; and the Nundi is in a pretty detached building in the court. These objects, with the choultries and some cottages, are opposite to my tent door, and nothing but the intense heat prevents me from walking among such beautiful scenery; but though not a sun-beam passes through the shade under which we are encamped, it is impossible to think of taking any exercise till near sunset.

Great Cave at Carli, Dec. 17th 1809.—I am told that we are now at least six thousand feet above the level of the sea, and the greatest part of that height we have ascended to-day. We left Compowli in the dark at five o'clock, and reached the foot of the ghaut at sunrise. The ascent was so steep and rugged, that I soon left my palankeen, and with one of my companions walked up the mountain. It is impossible to describe the exquisite beauty of the landscape. High mountains and bold projecting rocks, overhang deep woods of trees unknown to Europeans. Flowering shrubs of most delicious perfumes, and creeping-plants of every various hue, form natural bowers as they hang from tree to tree, and now shewing, now concealing the distant ocean, delight the eye at every step; while here and there an opening like a lawn, with herds of antelopes, makes you forget that the tiger prowls through the overhanging forest, and that the serpent lurks beneath the many-coloured bower.

At Condowli, a pretty village just above the ghaut, the hamauls stopped to bathe and drink, and to claim the fee for coming up the mountain, which is a sheep; it costs from one to two rupees, and is divided between the twelve hamauls, who belong to one palankeen, for very few Hindoos abstain entirely from animal food, although none eat of the cow or of the hog. Here I got into my palankeen, and went on to the foot of the hill where the cave of Carli is situated. As it was near twelve o'clock when we reached the village below the cave, we heartily wished that we had ordered our breakfast to await us there, for we had half a mile to climb up a rugged rock on foot, in the eye of the mid-day sun of India; and having tasted nothing since dinner yesterday, we were so exhausted when we reached it, that we could hardly raise our eyes to observe the wonders of the cavern.

When at length we looked round, we almost fancied ourselves in a Gothic cathedral. Instead of the low flat roof of the cave of Elephanta, this rises to an astonishing height, with a highly coved roof, supported by twenty-one pillars on each side, and terminating in a semicircle. Opposite to the entrance is a large temple (if I may call it so,) not hollowed, with a dome, on which is fixed a huge teak umbrella, as a mark of respect. Without the pillars there is a kind of aisle on each side of about six feet wide; the length of the cave is forty paces, and its breadth is fourteen. Here are no sculptures within the cavern except on the capitals of the pillars. The columns are mostly hexagons, though the number of angles varies; the bases are formed like compressed cushions; the capitals resemble an inverted flower, or a bell, on the top of which are two elephants, with two riders on each; and on several of the columns there are inscriptions in a character not hitherto decyphered. There is a very curious circumstance in this cavern, which is, that the roof is ribbed with teak wood, cut to fit the cove exactly, and supported by teeth in the timber fitting to corresponding holes in the rock; I imagine this to be a precaution against the destruction of this beautiful work by the monsoon rains. The cave of Carli is really one of the most magnificent chambers I ever saw, both as to proportion and workmanship. It is situated near the top of a wooded mountain, commanding one of the finest prospects in the world; its reser-

M.G. del. Etch'd by James Storer.

Interior of the Great Cave at Carli.

Pub^d by A. Constable & Co. Edinburgh June 1 1822.

M.G. del.

Etch'd. by James Storer.

Entrance to the Great Cave of Carli.

Pub^{d}. by A. Constable & Co. Edinburgh, June 1.1812.

voirs cut, like itself, out of the living rock, overflow with the purest water, and the country around it is fertile enough to supply every thing in abundance for human subsistence. The cave is a temple, and on each side there are corridores, with cells proper for the residence of priests and their families. But the most laboured part of the work is the portico of the temple. One-third of its height is filled up by a variety of figures, one of which, in a dancing posture, is remarkable for gracefulness of design, and the ends are occupied to the same height by gigantic elephants; above these is a cornice of reeds, bound together by fillets at equal distances, and the space over it is filled by small arched niches, finished with the same cornice. The centre is occupied by a horse-shoe arch, with a pointed moulding above, and below there is a square door of entrance to the cave. To protect the portico from the injuries of the weather, a rude screen was left at the entrance, part of which has fallen in; before it there is an enormous pillar, crowned with three animals, and now overgrown with moss and grass.

The difference between the cavern temples of Carli and of Elephanta is striking. Here are no personifications of the deity, no separate cells for secret rites; and the religious opinions which consecrated them are no less different. The cave of Carli is a temple dedicated to the religion of the Jines, a sect whose antiquity is believed by some to be greater than that of the Braminical faith, from which their tenets are essentially different, though many of their customs agree entirely with those of the Bramins, as might be expected from natives of the same country.

As the Braminical books represent the history of the gods as a series of awatars or descents, the Jine worship supposes men raised to the rank of divinities; but unlike the deified heroes of other nations, it is not on the warrior, but on the contemplative sage, that it bestows immortality; thus, besides the Great Deity, answering to the *Brehm* of the Bramins, the Jines worship their twenty-four first *Gooroos*, or spiritual teachers. They describe God as all-wise, all-seeing, all-productive, all-happy, without name, without relation, without shape, immortal; he is exempt from ignorance, mental blindness, name, tribe, love, and weakness. The man who attains to these perfections, and overcomes these evils, obtains, 1st, A station for beholding God at a distance; 2d, He is in the presence of God; 3d, He is equal in likeness to God; and, 4th, He becomes united to God, or rather is absorbed into the divine essence, when he is adored. The Jines have fourteen sacred books in the Sanscrit and Pracreat languages. It is not ascertained whether some of these be not also used by the Bramins; if so, they are probably such as concern the sciences, for the great reproach which they throw on the Bramins is, that they are hearers, that is, believers, of the fables of the Vedas.

The Jines believe that the world is of itself eternal, and that its changes are the effects of necessity. They hold, that to abstain from slaughter is grace, and that to kill any thing is sin. They accordingly abstain from animal food, from the fruit of trees giving milk, and from honey. Adultery and theft are forbidden; they burn the dead, and throw their ashes into the water, but pay no honours to the deceased. They are divided into four classes, but in what respects they agree with or differ from the Braminical castes I have not learnt; like the Bramins, they worship fire, and have sixteen ceremonies in common with them.

The Jines once possessed a large and powerful kingdom, under several dynasties of kings; but their long and violent wars against the Braminical powers of India, had exceedingly reduced them, when the Mahomedan kings of Beejnugger destroyed them as a nation, about the thirteenth century, and since that time they have only existed in a few detached bodies, extremely shy of confessing their religion. The few Jines I have seen seem poor and miserable; their appearance is like that of the other natives of India: the *poroohit* or priests do not shave their heads, nor do they wear a turban. The priests are all subject to the Gooroo of Sravana Bellagoola, where the most sacred temples of the Jines now exist; they were built by Rajah Nulla, a Jine king of Madura; the first of that name reigned A. D. 776-800, and the second A. D. 900. Great part of the revenues of these temples were confiscated by Hyder-Ally, and the East India Company has still further impoverished them, by selling part of the lands which maintained them. The principal stations of the remaining Jines are at Pennaconda, Conjeveram, Dehli, and Collapore *.

But to return to my Journal. While we were all seated at breakfast, we were surprised by the entrance of a Choabdar, that is, a servant who attends on persons of consequence, runs before them with a silver stick, and keeps silence at the doors of their apartments, from which last office he derives his name. He came to announce the arrival of Mr ——, the British resident at the court of Poonah, who, hearing of our intention to visit that capital, had come so far to meet us; and as neither he nor any

* *Pennaconda*, on a branch of the Godavery, called Narsipoor river, lies in 15° 30′ N. lat. and 80° 50′ E. long. Collapore, in Berar, is in 20° 55′ N. lat. and 78° 10′ E. long. Dehli, on the Jumna, is in 28° 42′ N. lat. and 77° 8′ E. long. Conjeveram, celebrated for its Hindoo pagodas, as well as for its Jina antiquities, is in 12° 50′ N. lat. and 79° 40′ E. long.

of his party had visited the caves of Carli before, we examined them together. To some of the caves on the right of the great temple we ascended by winding steps in the rock, now almost worn away, and to others still higher, by ladders which the priests had placed for us. These chambers are square, having cells round them, each cell about ten feet by six, and at one end a high bench or bed-place is left in the stone; in front of the largest there is an open corridor, ornamented with pillars resembling those at Elephanta; the others are only lighted by windows cut in the rock. To the left of the great temple the small caves are occupied by the wives and children of the priests, who live in a little modern building close to them; and, not thinking it right to disturb them merely to gratify our curiosity, we did not visit their chambers. We shall remain in the cave till the cool of the day, when we shall descend the hill by a longer path than that by which we came up, to meet our palankeens, and shall then join the resident's party at the village of Carli, where there is a large tank and a good bazar. The hamlet at the foot of the hill, though two miles nearer, is less convenient, as it is almost in ruins, and its tank and pagoda are in a state of melancholy decay; it is named Ekvera, and the cave is often called by the same name. There are some other caverns begun in the hill, but none have yet been seen that are finished.

Tulligong, Dec. 18.—We came this stage of eighteen miles to breakfast. The scene at decamping in the morning was very picturesque; our people had lighted great fires among the trees to see to strike the tents and to pack the furniture; every thing was in motion; already half the bullocks and kootis were on their march; some of the palankeens had also left the camp, and we saw them by the light of their torche long after the songs of the bearers were out of hearing; the lascars were striking the last of the tents, and the very horses seemed impatient to begin the journey. The morning air was really cold, but as the sun rose it became so hot, that, after riding ten miles, I was obliged to get into my palankeen. The country through which we passed is dreary and bleak; it is only where a village grove rises here and there, that the sameness of a moor-like plain, with distant hills, is interrupted. The grains I saw were mostly gram * and bageree †, but near one of the villages there were some fine fields of wheat.

Round Tulligong the country presents melancholy traces of the ravages of war and famine. The camps of Scindia and Holkar are everywhere discernible, and the march of their soldiers is marked by ruined houses and temples, and drained tanks. Tulligong is just recovering from the effects of the dreadful famine of 1805-6. It is said that, in this town alone, eighty thousand persons perished; and one of my fellow-travellers says, that when he was here last year, the bones strewed the fields around. The inhabitants of many towns and villages emigrated, hoping to find elsewhere that sustenance which failed at home; thousands perished on the road side, and many, at the very moment when they stretched forth their hands to receive the means of life which the charity of the British afforded, sunk to death ere the long wished-for morsel reached their lips. A mother, with five child-

* Gram, a kind of pea, which is used as provender for cattle.

† Bageree, a coarse grain, of which the natives make a cake resembling barley-meal bannocks.

ren, on her way from Hydrabad to Bombay, had reached Salsette; there she was too weak to proceed, and, to preserve herself and four of her offspring, she sold the fifth for a little rice; but it was too late; she and her infants perished the next morning; and instances of the like were numerous. Yet such was the patience of the Hindoos, that they saw the waggons of rice sent by the English at Bombay to the relief of Poonah, pass through their villages without an attempt to stop them.

But the fields of Tulligong are again cultivated, new houses are rising to replace the old ones, and the town seems full of children. We visited the Rajah Cunterow-Teravaly-Sinhaputty, who is hereditary general of the Mahratta forces, and his family held other great offices; but they are now superseded in the Peishwa's favour, and the general has nothing of his former consequence but the name, and a huge state elephant which is kept at his palace gate. He is the guardian of the pagoda; and by his permission we were furnished with excellent fish from the tank. The Rajah is a plump stupid-looking man, but good-natured and hospitable. He begged our friends to let the children visit him, for he had never seen an European child, and the Mahrattas say proverbially, when they would praise beauty, "As lovely as a "white child." Our encampment is on the side of the tank, half a mile from the town; the scenery is pretty, but not to be compared with that at Compowli and Chowk.

Chimchore, Dec. 19, 1809.—I have just seen what I thought I should never have met with on this side of Thibet, namely, an *alive god,* called the Deo of Chimchore, who is nothing less than Ganesa himself, incarnate in the person of a boy of twelve years old, the eighth of his family honoured as the vehicle of the deity's appearance on earth. The first was Maraba, a Gosseyn, whose piety was so exemplary, that Ganesa rewarded it by becoming incarnate in his person, at the same time committing to his care a sacred stone, and the guardianship of his own temple, promising the same favours to his descendants for seven generations. These are now passed away; but as the piety and superstition of the Deo's neighbours has enriched the family by grants of lands, and towns, and villages, the holy Bramins have decreed, that the god is still incarnate in the family of Maraba; and to the objection that the promise was only to seven generations, they answer, that as the deity was able to grant that favour to the seven immediate descendants of the holy Gosseyn, it would be impious to doubt his power of continuing it to their posterity. The Deo's palace or *bara* is an enormous pile of building, without any kind of elegance, near the river Mootha, on which the town stands. As we entered the court, we saw a number of persons engaged in the honourable and holy office of mixing the sacred cow-dung to be spread on the floors of the bara. The whole palace looked dirty, and every window was crowded with sleek well-fed Bramins, who doubtless take great care of the Deo's revenues. We found his little godship seated in a mean viranda, on a low wooden seat, not any way distinguished from other children, but by an anxious wildness of the eyes, said to be occasioned by the quantity of opium which he is daily made to swallow. He is not allowed to play with other boys, nor is he permitted to speak any language but Sanscrit, that he may not converse with any but the Bramins. He received us very politely, said he was always pleased to see English people; and after some conversation, which a Bramin interpreted, we took leave, and were presented by his divine hand with almonds and sugar-candy perfumed with asafœtida, and he received in return a handful of rupees.

From the bara we went to the tombs of the former Deos, which are so many small temples inclosed in a well paved court, planted round with trees, communicating with the river by a handsome flight of steps. Here was going on all the business of worship. In one place were women pouring oil, water, and milk over the figures of the gods; in another children decking them with flowers; here devotees and pilgrims performing their ablutions, and there priests chaunting portions of the vedas; yet all going on in a manner that might beseem the inhabitants of the Castle of Indolence. As I passed one of the tomb-temples, I caught a glimpse of a large highly-polished stone, which I suppose is the Palladium of Chimchore, but I was desired not to approach it, so that I could not gratify my curiosity. I returned to our tents, filled with reflections not very favourable to the dignity of human nature, after witnessing such a degrading instance of superstitious folly. If I could be assured that the communication with Europe would in ever so remote a period free the natives of India from their moral and religious degradation, I could even be almost reconciled to the methods by which the Europeans have acquired possession of the country.

Our tents are opposite to the Deo's bara, on the other side of the river, in a grove of mango, banian, pepil, and babool trees *.

* " *Acacia Arabica,* in Hindui *Babul,* in Sanscrit *Burbura.* The gum is called *Babulka Gund.* The *Acacia vera,* or *Mimosa Nilotica,* which produces the gum-arabic, is not found among the numerous species of Acacia that are natives of Hindostan; but the gum of the babul is so perfectly similar to gum-arabic, that for every purpose, whether medicinal or economical, it may be substituted for it. The bark of the tree

The scene before us is beautiful; the town towards the river is a groupe of temples, in whose courts are magnificent trees, overhanging flights of steps of hewn stone, which lead to the river, and on which you see crowds of people coming from or going to the bath.

Sungum Poonah, Dec. 20.—We arrived here last night at five o'clock. The residency is two miles from Poonah, at the junction of the rivers Moolha and Mootha, on which account it is called the *Sungum* or junction. The apartments are a groupe of *bungalos* or garden-houses, placed in a most delightful garden, where the apple, the pear, and the peach, the orange, the almond, and the fig, overshadow the strawberry, and are hedged in by the rose, the myrtle, and the jasmin.

When dinner was announced we assembled in the garden; two choabdars walked before the resident, to make way for the great man, according to the oriental custom; but he dispenses with the ceremony of their proclaiming his titles as he walks into his own apartments. The dining bungalo is close to the river, on a little height; the view from its windows is very pretty; to the right is Poonah, surrounded with gardens on the banks of

like that of most of the Acacias, is a powerful astringent, and is used instead of oak-bark for tanning, by the European manufacturers of leather in Bengal."—*Catalogue of Indian Medicinal Plants and Drugs, by* JOHN FLEMING, M. D.

The flower of the Babul is a bright yellow ball, very sweet-scented, and the wood is both hard and tough; it is the best in India for wheels and axle-trees, and grows in great abundance all over the Deckan.

the river; to the left is the place where the suttees* are performed, rendered picturesque by a number of tombs of a very pretty style of architecture, and a few trees; and the whole country round is highly cultivated. It was late ere we left the dining-room, for our party was such as does not often assemble in India. For once we forgot rupees and bales of cotton, and enjoyed a flow of polished conversation, rational cheerfulness, and urbanity, which it would be ungrateful not to mention, and which it is impossible to forget.

We experienced some disappointment this morning, for we were to have seen and conversed with a Nusteek philosopher, who sent word that he was too ill to come to us. These sages are abhorred by the Bramins, who call them atheists, because they assert that the soul can be assured of nothing but its own existence, and that therefore we cannot be certain whether there be a God or no. The books of this sect are proscribed, nor dare any Bramin give or lend them, or even discover where they may be found. The Vedantis are not so unfavourably thought of; they deny the existence of matter, and affirm that our life is the effect of *Maya* or delusion, produced by *Brehm*, the eternal energy; they compare it to a glass bubble filled with water, floating on the ocean; when the bubble bursts, the water is lost in its parent source; so, when the delusion of existence ends, man is as if he had never been. A Pundit of this sect, to whom I once mentioned Bishop Berkeley's system, smiled, and, alluding to the popular belief, said, He must have been a Vedanti Bramin in his pre-existent state.

* *Suttees,* the burning of Hindoo women with their husbands.

But I must leave these eastern speculations, and return to objects of common sight and hearing. To-day, for the first time, I rode on an elephant; his motions are by no means unpleasant, and they are quick enough to keep a horse at a round trot to keep up with him. The animal we rode is eleven feet high; his forehead and ears are beautifully mottled; his tusks are very thick, and sawed off to a convenient length for him to kneel while his riders mount. On his back an enormous pad is placed, and tightly girt with chains and cotton rope; upon this is placed the *howda*, a kind of box divided into two parts; the front containing a seat large enough for two or three persons, and the back a space for the servant who bears the umbrella. The driver sits astride on the animal's neck, and with one foot behind each ear he guides him as he pleases. On our return we saw him fed; as soon as the howda is taken off, he is led to the water, where he washes and drinks; he is then fastened by the heels to a peg in his stable, where he lies down to sleep for a few hours in the night only. His food is rice, grass, leaves, and young branches of trees, but he is most fond of bread and fruit, especially the plantain. Our evening excursion was to see the ground prepared for the new palace, to be built for the Peishwa by the British, his highness paying for the same. The design is handsome; but I have some doubts as to the propriety of a Grecian building for the residence of a Mahratta Bramin. The site and ground-plan are already marked out, and consecrated, by being plastered over with the sacred compost of cow-dung and ashes.

Dec. 21.—This morning the gentlemen of our party joined those of the residency in a fox-chase, a favourite amusement of the young Englishmen here, although the heat always obliges them to quit the field by nine o'clock. The great sport of the Mahrattas is ram-fighting. The animals are trained for the purpose, and some of them which we saw were really beautiful; but as these were not spectacles for ladies, we dismissed them without a combat, much to the disappointment of their owners, whose fondness for these shews is only exceeded by their love of gambling, which so possesses the Hindoos, that they sometimes play away their wives and children, and even their own liberty. In the afternoon the resident escorted us through the town of Poonah, to the sacred mount of Parbutty or Parvati, about two miles from Poonah. On each side of the road are gardens, fields, and country-houses; and at the foot of Parbutty the Peishwa has a pleasant palace, with extensive gardens, in which there is a beautifully winding lake, whose banks are clothed with trees; and in the middle of the bason, opposite to the palace, is a small island with a temple, and two or three Bramins' houses, in a grove of fruit-trees.

Near a pretty bridge which crosses the lake, we got off the elephant, and ascended the hill by a handsome flight of stone steps. Near the top are six small brass guns for firing on festivals, and a little way above there are temples to various gods, which we were permitted to enter, but they contained only the common coarse gods, and pictures equally void of taste and design, executed in gaudy colours, on the walls. The temple of Parbutty, which crowns the hill, we were not allowed to approach, nearer than the outer gate, so that we saw nothing but the Nundi in the court. The view from Parbutty is fine; it commands the town, with its gardens and plantations, the cantonments of the British subsidiary force, and the Sungum. Near the foot of the hill is a large square field inclosed with high brick walls, where the Peishwa assembles the Bramins, to whom he gives alms at the great Mahratta feast at the close of the rainy season. They are shut up in it till all are assembled, and as they come out one by one, they receive the gratuity, of which, but for this precaution, some would get too many shares. On this occasion the Bramins come from all parts of India, and beg their way to and from Poonah, so that they have the pleasure of the festival, and gain a few rupees by their journey.

I am sorry the Peishwa is now absent on a pilgrimage, as I should like to see a native prince. I am told that he is a man of little or no ability, a great sensualist, and very superstitious. His time is spent in making pilgrimages, or buried in his zenana. Hardly a week passes without some devout procession, on which he squanders immense sums, and consequently he is always poor.

The Peishwa's family is Braminical, but of so low an order that the pure Bramins refused to eat with him; and at Nassuck, a place of pilgrimage near the source of the Godavery, the Peishwa was not allowed to descend into the water by the same flight of steps used by the holy priests. This enviable privilege the predecessors of the Peishwa had been endeavouring to obtain ever since the year 1726; but he lately threatened to give up the holy temple for a barrack for the English soldiers, in case of the further obstinacy of the Bramins, who, to save their gods from pollution, have at length granted to their master the whole of the privileges of their order. We returned from Parbutty through the town. I saw nothing to distinguish the bazar of the capital from those of the villages, excepting a greater number of female ornaments. The houses are very mean, only the better ones are painted as in Bombay. As we went along, I saw a number of women pouring jugs of water before a door, and was told it was the custom to do so when a child (I think only the first) is born, as an emblem of fertility. The ancient palace, or rather castle of Poonah, is surrounded by high thick walls, with four large towers, and has only one entrance, through a highly pointed arch; here the Peishwa's brother and other members of his family reside; but he has built a modern house for himself in another part of the town. It is square, with four turrets, and is painted all over with pale green leaves. We stopped opposite to the windows, and saw several of the Peishwa's ladies. One of them was pointed out as the reigning favourite. She was the wife of one of his Highness's subjects, and had the reputation of being the most beautiful woman in his dominions, on which account he sent for her to court, and took her to himself. After making our salams before the palace, we returned to the Sungum, crossing the river a little below the wooden bridge, for though in the rainy season the Moolha is a large river, it is now scarcely knee-deep.

Dec. 22.—We took a long and beautiful ride through the country this morning; but the scenes of nature, however charming to the eye, must tire in description, for want of a sufficient variety and precision in the language we must use. We visited some small excavations near the Sungum, which I should have admired more, had I not seen those of Carli and of Elephanta. They are below the plain, and not visible till one is within them. We entered through a natural cleft in a low rock, and found ourselves in a small area, in the centre of which is a round temple, with six pillars, containing the Nundi; beyond it is a square cave, supported by several plain pillars, which do not appear to have been finished. Compartments in the sides of the cavern seem to have been designed for figures, but we found no gods, excepting a small figure of Hanuman, which seems to have been lately placed there, and before which lay some dry flowers and leaves.

Panwell, Dec. 26.—We left Poonah on the 23d, at day-break, and arrived here yesterday afternoon. As we returned by the same road that we travelled before, we had nothing new to see, and therefore we only stopped as long as was absolutely necessary at each stage. As we were walking down the ghaut, we met several horsemen from Scind and Guzerat, on their road to Poonah, in search of military service. They were very handsomely dressed and accoutred, and were walking, while their horses, richly caparisoned, were led. Their arms are swords, shields, and spears, painted and gilt. One warrior had a bow and arrows; his bow hung by his side, in a case covered with tissue; his arrows were light and delicately made, the heads of various shapes, pointed, barbed, or cut into crescents, and his quiver, slung over his shoulder, glittered with gilding and foil. When we reached Panwell our tents were not arrived, so that we were obliged to keep Christmas-day in the Mahomedan saint's tomb; luckily the apathy of the Mussulmans prevented their being offended. I am delighted at having accomplished this visit to the Mahratta country; for though there is little interesting in Poonah itself, yet, as the capital of a nation whose period of glory, bright and short, is so recent, it is at least an object of curiosity.

Till the time of Sevajee, Poonah was an inconsiderable village, but during his reign it became the capital of the Mahratta states, and has since continued so*.

Shahjee, the father of Sevajee, was descended from the ancient Ranas of Oodipore, but was himself an adventurer, and the son of an exile, who was a common horseman, in the service of one of the Mahomedan kings of the Deckan. By his intrigues and talents he raised himself to consideration, and became agent to one of the last of the Nizam Shahs. Being besieged in Caliane by the enemies of his master, and reduced to the greatest extremities, he fled to Bejapore, and left his wife in the hands of the enemy. Shortly afterwards his son, Sevajee, was born, and sent to Poonah, then an inconsiderable village, where Shahjee had a house, and where he was carefully brought up by a Bramin. At the age of nineteen, Shahjee being then employed in the service of Bejapoor, Sevajee seized his treasures, and, collecting a body of troops, began those incursions by which he harassed the neighbouring powers, and at length raised the Mahrattas to their highest glory. The miserable condition of the five Mahomedan kingdoms that had established themselves upon the ruins of the Bhamanee monarchy †, was ex-

* Lieutenant-Colonel Mackenzie, of the Madras establishment, informed me that, long before the Mahomedan conquest of India, a little commonwealth of Arabs existed on or near the spot where Poonah now stands. Whether they were pirates, or resorted there for the purposes of commerce, is not ascertained.

† The Bhamanee dynasty of Deckanee kings begins with Sultaun Alla O'Dien Houssein Kangoh Bhamanee, A. H. 748, A. D. 1347. Koolburga was new named by him Ahssunabad, and became his capital. The name Bhamanee is derived from Kangoh, a Bramin, who had been the benefactor of Alla O'Dien, and was the first Hindoo who became the minister of a Mussulman prince. A century had scarcely elapsed when the kingdom was embroiled in civil dissensions, and was finally split into five different monarchies, founded by the great officers of state. These were the

tremely favourable to his enterprizes, and he succeeded in it notwithstanding every effort of Aurengzebe, then newly established on the throne of Dehli, to prevent him. His first conquests were the hill forts, situated among the ghauts, places of strength adapted for receiving his plunder and securing his women, during his incursions into the adjacent country. His troops consisted of light and swift horsemen, and were always ready, on the cessation of the rains, to plunder, before any army could be assembled to oppose them. In this manner he twice pillaged Surat, carrying off immense treasures. At length, however, partly by force and partly by stratagem, he was obliged to yield himself up to Aurengzebe, and, with his son Sambajee, was carried prisoner to Dehli, whence he soon found means to escape. He had established a custom of distributing among the populace immense quantities of confectionaries, which were brought in large baskets. After continuing this practice for some weeks, he concealed his son in one of those baskets, and himself in another, and ordering a slave to lie down in his bed and counterfeit sickness, he thus left his prison. Sambajee was entrusted to the care of an old Bramin, who conveyed him in safety to Rairi, where Sevajee soon joined them, after passing through Muttra, Benares, and Ghya. After this adventure he recovered all the forts he had lost, and acquired new possessions, particularly in the Kokun, or low coun-

Adil Shahee, established at Beejapoor,	-	A. H. 895, A. D. 1489.
Nizam Shahee, at Ahmednuggur,	-	A. H. 895, A. D. 1489.
Kuttoob Shahee, at Golconda,	-	A. H. 918, A. D. 1512.
Bureed Shahee, at Bider,	}	About A. D. 1540.
Ommaid Shahee, in part of Berar,		

All these monarchies were subdued by Aurengzebe, and most of their kings were either put to death or imprisoned for life by that conqueror.

try, between the ghaut and the sea, besides the ports of Dundra-Rajepoor, Sevendroog, and Coulaba.

About 1668, we find Poonah mentioned as the residence of Sevajee, where he received his father Shahjee with great respect and affection, not even sitting down in his presence; and where, in 1674, his coronation took place, and he first struck coins in his own name. Three or four years afterwards he made an incursion into the Carnatic, where his brother Ekojee had made himself an independent kingdom, passed near Madras, and took Ginjee; but on the whole his success was inconsiderable, though he carried off a great booty.

Sevajee died at Rairi, A. D. 1680. His character is very striking. Born in an obscure station, he not only raised himself to the command of a powerful people, but he actually made the nation he governed; and although the Mogul arms were employed against him for nineteen years, he continued to advance his own projects, and ultimately succeeded. It must be confessed, that he employed treachery to forward many of his designs; but his enterprizes were always formed with sagacity, and executed with promptness and vigour. In modelling his government, he supposed the Mahratta state to be always at war, and the king at the head of his army; the affairs of the state were to be conducted by a *Prudhee Nedhee*, or viceroy, and eight *Pradhans* or counsellors, the first of which was the Peishwa; these ministers were to be chosen from all ranks of people, and removeable at will.

Under Sambajee, the son and successor of Sevajee, the consequence of the Mahrattas continued to increase; the greater part of the Kokun was subdued, forts were built, and the Mahratta fleet sustained two or three naval engagements with the Siddees, then in the service of the Mogul. In the midst of this good fortune, Sambajee was surprised by the artifices of Aurengzebe, and murdered with tortures. He was succeeded by his brother Rama, during whose reign the Mahrattas maintained their character and conquests, although they met with some severe checks from the Mussulmans. On the death of Rama, Shahoo, the son of Sambajee, succeeded to the throne, and in his reign began the degradation of the house of Sevajee, and the rise of the power of the Peishwas.

Cannojee Angria, a pirate, having made himself master of several sea-ports in the Kokun, Shahoo sent the Peishwa Balajee Wiswunaut to treat with, or to conquer him. He preferred the former, brought Angria to a peaceable agreement with the Mahratta court respecting his forts and ships; and, from his success in this negotiation, he became the chief director of the Mahratta affairs. Shahoo remained shut up in the fortress of Sitarrah, while Balajee held his court at Poonah, and by his victories obliged the Mogul ministers to consent to the payment of the *chout* or fourth, and the *desmookhee* or tenth of the produce of the Deckan to the Mahrattas. Balajee was succeeded in the Peishwaship by his son Bajee Rao Bulal, during whose government the families of Scindia and Holkar first distinguished themselves. In 1735, Bajee Rao Bulal was succeeded by his son Balajee Bajee Rao; and the same year his other son, Ragonaut Rao, with Mulhar Rao Holkar and Dulajee Scindiah, ravaged the whole of the Mogul empire, pillaging Dehli, Agra, and Lahore, overrunning Bengal and the Bundlecund, and seizing Berar and Orissa, while Gwyckwar, another Mahratta, took possession of Guzerat. Meantime the Rajah Shahoo died, and was succeeded in his prison of Sitarrah, A. D. 1749, by Rajah Ram Rajah, in whose reign the Mahrattas, not content with ravaging the northern provinces of India, descended from their mountains like torrents, and poured into the Carnatic and Mysore, under Ragonaut Rao, and his nephew Mhadoo Rao, who had succeeded his father Balajee Bajee Rao in the Peishwaship. It was against these chiefs that *Hyder Naïk* made his first campaigns, and perhaps the whole splendour of his military career is owing to their invasion of his country, which called forth the hitherto dormant energies of his mind. While the Peishwa's army was engaged in the south, the Mahratta forces under Sadasho Bhow, Wiswas Rao, and Junkojee Scindiah, were defeated with incredible slaughter at Paniput *, A. D. 1761, by Ahmed Shah, the Mogul general; and this defeat, together with the check the southern army met with from Hyder, seems to have given the deathblow to the Mahratta conquests.

In 1772, Mhadoo Rao was succeeded by Narryn Rao, who was shortly afterwards murdered by his uncle Ragonaut Rao, commonly called Raghabhoy. The Mahratta chiefs refused obedience to a murderer, and a civil war ensued, when the English supported Raghabhoy, but ineffectually. Tukojee Holkar, and Mahajee Scindia, declared themselves independent, and the son of Narryn Rao was made Peishwa, but was shortly after accidentally killed.

The present Peishwa is the son of Raghabhoy, whom the victories and intrigues of the English have placed on the Musnud, and have reduced to a state little more enviable than that of the prisoner Rajah at Sitarrah, who is the grandson of Sevajee. The Peishwa still keeps up the farce of going to Sitarrah to receive

* Paniput is in 29° 23′ N. lat. and 76° 50′ E. long. and is 40 geographical miles from Delhi.

the insignia of his office from the hand of the Rajah, but is himself so completely under our dominion, that he pays a subsidy to maintain the three thousand troops which surround his capital and keep him a priscner.

Pointe de Galle, Island of Ceylon, Feb. 16, 1810.—Having been very unwell for some time, I was advised to take a short voyage for the recovery of my health. This is a remedy which seldom fails in this climate, and is found particularly useful in the intermittent fevers of the country. Accordingly, as some of our friends were sailing for England, we thought we could not do better than accompany them thus far on their passage.

We came here in an eight hundred ton country-ship, where every thing is as new to me as if I had never been on board of a large vessel before. All the sailors are lascars, and the only Europeans are the captain, three officers, and the surgeon; the gunners and quarter-masters, of whom there are ten, are Indian Portuguese; they are called *secunnies.* The best lascars are Siddees, a tribe of Mahomedans, inhabitants of Gogo in Guzerat. They live chiefly on rice and salt fish, but occasionally they take tea, sugar, and fruit, as preventives or cures for the scurvy. The ship is built of teak-wood, which lasts much longer than oak; it does not shrink, so that little caulking is required; and it contains so much oil, that the iron bolts and nails driven into it do not rust; it is however inconveniently heavy. The masts are of poon, which, though lighter than the teak, is cumbrous compared with European timber. The rigging is of coier rope, which is made of the coco-nut husk, steeped till the woody part decays, when the fibres are beaten, washed, and laid by hand, as they are too stiff to be spun. The coier rope is very strong, and does not shrink; fresh water rots it, so that the standing rigging is served over with wax-cloth and hempen-yarn; but salt water preserves it, and coier cables are found to answer particularly well. Another kind of rope, brought from Manilla, is both softer and stronger; it is made from the long fibres of the stalk of a species of wild plantain. Hempen rope is also made in India, and canvas of excellent quality is manufactured in Bengal from the hemp * which grows plentifully all over Hindostan, but of which one-third is lost for want of proper management.

We were seventeen days on the passage from Bombay to Pointe de Galle, during which time we had very fine weather, with land and sea breezes. In crossing the gulf of Manar, between Cape Comorin and Ceylon, we experienced the usual fresh winds, which blow in or out of the gulf according to the season. The appearance of the land about this place is beautiful; the hills and valleys, mountains and woods, with the projecting rocks about the road-stead, the old Dutch fort, and the shipping, make a most delightful landscape. We had scarcely anchored when we

* "*Cannabis sativa*; in Hindui, *Bhang* and *Canja*; in Sanscrit, *Gunjica*. Lamarck is of opinion, that the Indian Ganja is a different species of Cannabis from the *Cannabis sativa*, and names it 'Cannabis Indica foliis alternis,' (Encyc. Bot. I. 695). But Wildenow, after remarking that the *European* species has also alternate leaves, assures us, that, on comparing it with many specimens of the *Indian* plant, he could not perceive any difference between them. See Sp. Pl. IV. 763. Neither could Dr Roxburgh, on comparing plants raised from *Europe* hemp-seed with the Ganja plant, discover in the latter the slightest distinction, not even enough on which to found a variety."—*A Catalogue of Indian Medicinal Plants and Drugs, by* JOHN FLEMING, M. D. *Calcutta*, 1810.

were surrounded by a number of little boats, containing vegetables, fruit, and bread. These boats are curiously constructed; a hollow tree forms the bottom, in the shape of a canoe; on each side of this a plank is sewed with coier thread, and the interstices are filled up with dammar; across the boat two poles are fixed, to one end of which, at the distance of twice the breadth of the boat, an outrigger is fastened to balance the boat, and to prevent its oversetting. On one of these poles the mast of bamboo is usually set up; an old mat, or a piece of coarse cotton, serves as a sail, and the rudder is an oar or paddle, sometimes tied to the boat, but oftener held by its master. The fishermen and boatmen of Ceylon are chiefly Mahomedans, called *Moplahs*, from the Malabar coast.

Pointe de Galle is an old Dutch fort, very much out of repair, and not worth making better. It is very neatly kept, and has a cheerful air from the rows of trees planted on each side of the streets. There are not above six English families resident here, but at present a much greater number are collected, as the fleet assembles here for convoy, and to take in spices on the voyage home. I walked to the beach this morning, to see the last of the homeward-bound ships; two-and-twenty sail got under way at day-break, and many an anxious wish went with them. Many a mother had trusted her darling child to the waves, nay, much more, to the care of strangers, in the conviction that, depriving herself of the delight of watching over it, was to secure its permanent advantage. And many a fond husband, unable to accompany his wife, had sent her to breathe her native air, as the last resource to preserve a life so dear.

Feb. 18.—We intended to have left Pointe de Galle yesterday, but were prevailed on to make an excursion to see a celebrated Bhudhist temple at Bellegam, about twenty miles south-east from this place. None but open carriages are used in Ceylon; we therefore went in *bandies*, in plain English *gigs*, to the village of Bellegam, where we breakfasted in the rest-house on the sea-shore. At every station round the island there are rest-houses for travellers under the care of the *Modeliar*, or head-man of the place, in which are tables and chairs, but beds and table-furniture are provided by the travellers. As we accompanied one of the principal servants of government, the *Maha Modeliar*, or overseer of all the head-men of the island, attended us, and provided our breakfast; the table was covered with costly plate, which I found was all his property. The rest-house was decorated with white and coloured calico tied up in roses, and coco-nut leaves split so as to form fringes and festoons; the pillars of the viranda were covered with palm leaves tied up in bunches, and a gateway at a little distance was dressed in the manner of a triumphal arch, with leaves and many-coloured flowers.

After breakfast we walked to the temple, through some of the prettiest fields I have seen in India. A flight of rude stone steps leads to the building, which is low and mean, but near it are the ruins of an older and much handsomer structure. Opposite to the temple is a large solid conical building, supposed to cover the ashes of a Bhudhist saint, one of which ornaments the court of every temple to Bhud. Near it are two large trees, both sacred, one is the Pupil, a species of the banian, and the other bears large sweet-scented yellow flowers, something like a cistus.

Within the temple is a recumbent figure of Bhud, twenty-eight feet long; his countenance is broad and placid, his hair is curled like that of a negro, and on the crown of his head is a flame-like ornament, such as I have seen in Montfaucon and Denon, on the heads of the Egyptian deities.

The dress of the statue is like that of the priests of the temple, and, as well as the figure, is painted of a bright yellow colour, excepting a scarf which is red. Another Bhud is seated in a corner on a cobra-capella, coiled up as a seat, whose hood forms a canopy over his head. There is besides a gigantic four-handed statue of Vishnu, of a dark-blue colour, which appears to be of porcelain. The walls within the temple are covered with painted figures of Bhud, as they are called here, but which strongly resemble the Jine figures I have seen elsewhere; they are sitting with one leg over the knee of the other, and the fore-finger of the right hand applied to the thumb of the left, in the attitude of contemplation. The outer walls are painted with an immense number of figures, among which I noticed several exactly resembling one in Denon's 40th plate, of a conqueror holding the hair of a number of enemies at once with one hand, while the other is raised, apparently with the design of cutting off all the heads. The priests were all either unable or unwilling to give any explanation of these pictures, which appear to refer to the history or the mythology of the island, or both.

Among the Bhudhists there are no distinct castes; any man may obtain the honours of the priesthood who can read the common service of the temple, who has no bodily infirmity, who is strong enough to beg, and who will take a vow of celibacy; however, should he afterwards wish to marry, he is at liberty to do so on quitting the priesthood. These priests shave their heads entirely, and never cover them; they are clothed in yellow; the robe is very full, it is thrown over one shoulder, and leaves the other bare; they carry in their hands a small oval fan made of the leaf of the talipot, a species of palm. A spacious garden and some rice-fields belong to the temple, for the maintenance of the priests. The path from the temple to the garden crosses a shelving rock, on which there is an inscription, which neither the Maha Modeliar, who was with us, nor the priests, could read.

The sacred books of the Bhudhists are in the Pahli language, which it is said has a great resemblance to the Sanscrit, Pracreat, and Pehlavi tongues. Formerly there was an annual importation of books and priests from Siam, the great seat of Bhudhism; but of late years the intercourse between that country and Ceylon has nearly ceased, and the priests are consequently become extremely ignorant in the Cingalese territory; nor is it probable that those of the Candian country are much more enlightened, for the king being of a Hindoo family, Bhudhism has ceased to be the religion of the court, and is therefore much neglected.

The popular account of Bhudhism which follows, I regard with some distrust, as it reached me through the translations of some missionaries, who seem to have falsified, or at least exaggerated, some of the absurdities of that system, in order to obtain a stronger hold over the minds of their proselytes, very few of whom are learned enough to have recourse to their books in the originals for information, and therefore quietly acquiesce in the belief that Bhud and Satan are one and the same person; while their spiritual guides impress on their minds the sinfulness of worshipping the devil. Even the Maha Modeliar, who is a Dutch Protestant, though a man of sense, is so possessed with this idea, that he would fain have dissuaded us from going into the temple, where there were only some devils, as he called the images of the gods.

The Bhudhists are accused of absolutely denying the existence of a supreme being, and of looking to annihilation after death as supreme happiness; yet they have temples and a system of worship! They believe that there have been four Bhuds born in different ages and nations, to better the condition of mankind, by promulgating laws and destroying tyrants and oppressors. Having accomplished the benevolent end of their existence, they withdrew into woods and deserts, where they led lives of contemplation for thousands of years, and obtained command over millions of spirits who inhabit heaven and earth. The last Bhud is accounted the author of the sacred books, and of the present system of religion. He forbid the slaying of animals, either for food or sacrifice, and thus agrees in character with Bhud the ninth awatar of the Hindoo Vishnu. Like the Jines, the Bhudhists believe that, after death, the spirits of the virtuous will be raised through different degrees of happiness, with this difference, if my information be correct, that the Jines suppose *individual* existence to end by the absorption of the soul into the divine essence, while the Bhudhists believe in total annihilation as the consummation of felicity.

About two miles from the temple of Bellegam there is a large fragment of rock, on which is sculptured a figure twelve feet high; he appears armed, and one hand is held up and one down, as is usually seen in the statues of Vishnu. The country people call it the Cotta Rajah, who it seems was a conqueror from the main-land of India, but whose adventures are so blended with magical wonders, that I cannot venture to repeat them. An annual feast was formerly celebrated in honour of this figure, and in a small rock before it are holes, in which the Modeliar told me the people were wont to plant spears on that festival.

Although the village people are sufficiently accustomed to the sight of English travellers, as the governor or some of the superior officers of government go round the island twice or thrice a-year to inspect both its military and civil concerns, we had a crowd round us wherever we moved. The general appearance of the Cingalese is coarser than that of the natives of Bombay and the adjacent coast, and they wear less clothing in general. The Maha Modeliar being the principal native, I shall describe his dress first. Although a Christian, he conforms to the custom of his ancestors in wearing a piece of chintz wrapped round him like a petticoat, but the rest of his dress is in the Portuguese form. His stock and waistcoat of fine white cotton, are buttoned with rubies; his coat is of fine English broad-cloth, the buttons of embossed silver, and the button-holes embroidered with the same. Across his shoulders hangs a rich gold lace sword-belt, fastened with a cluster of precious stones; the sword hilt and scabbard are chassed gold, and the eyes and tongues of the lions heads on the hilt are of rubies. The Modeliar's hair is combed tight back from the face, and fastened in a knot behind; a square tortoiseshell comb ornaments the top of the head.

The common people wear their hair dressed in the same manner, excepting that the women deck the knot behind with long pins of gold and silver set with precious stones. Neither sex wears any clothing above the waist, excepting when they become household servants to Europeans, when they put on a jacket; the clothing of the better sort descends to the heels, the common people are only covered to the knee. The Cingalese houses are better constructed than those of the same class of natives in Bombay, owing perhaps to the necessities of the climate, which is more damp and variable. I am unwilling to think the natives of any country naturally inferior to those of another, and I therefore endeavour to account to myself for the great moral disparity between Europeans and Asiatics, by supposing that the severities of the northern climate, and the difficulty of raising food, give a spur to industry and invention, to surmount the disadvantages of nature, and to procure property and comforts, which are valued in proportion to the difficulty with which they are attained. But no such incitements to exertion exist in this climate, and the mind sinks in proportion to the inactivity of the body.

Schools for English, Dutch, and Cingalese, have been established in different parts of Ceylon. Those who are brought up in them are mostly baptized by the Dutch Protestant ministers, which opens to them small offices under government; hence they are becoming ambitious, and of course industrious. They build better houses, eat better food, and wear better clothes than their ancestors, and I am happy to find that their number is daily increasing.

We returned to Pointe de Galle late in the evening, and I was again charmed with the country we passed through. The road lies along the sea-shore, through coco-nut woods, in which there is here and there an opening, where you discover fields and lakes, forests and mountains, melting away in the distance. It became dark before we reached home, when suddenly the wood seemed in a blaze; eighteen or twenty of the inhabitants of a village, concealed by the brushwood, ran out of their houses with bundles of lighted coco-nut leaves, and preceded us to the next hamlet, where they were relieved by others, and so on to Pointe de Galle. The effect of this illumination surpassed that of any I ever saw. Sometimes the straight tall trunks of the palm-trees, whose fan-like heads remained in shadow, seemed to represent a magnificent colonade; sometimes, where the creeping plants had entwined themselves round them, and hung in festoons from tree to tree, they appeared like some enchanted bower, dressed by fairy hands; while the graceful figures of the torch-bearers, scarcely clothed, yet glittering with barbaric gold and pearl, with their joyous shouts, recalled to our imagination the triumphs of Bacchus.

This evening I went to see a little colony of Chinese near the fort; they were brought here by the government as gardeners; for none of the Europeans who have possessed Ceylon have yet been able to raise vegetables in the island; the patience of the Chinese has however succeeded, and I saw not only esculent vegetables of every kind, but thriving sugar-canes under their management. The gardeners have built themselves very neat houses in the garden. At each end of the principal room in every house there is a high table, over which is hung a tablet containing Chinese characters; I am told that these are the names of the forefathers of the families; and before each tablet a lamp was burning The rest of the furniture consisted of cane couches or beds, and pieces of carpet for covers, which are folded up in the day-time. At every door there were two or three chairs, and a low table with tea-pots and cups upon it. The dress and air of the Chinese is so exactly what we see on every China cup and dish, that it is needless to describe them.

Columbo, Feb. 28, 1810.—I am writing in a bungalo lent us by a friend, on the margin of the beautiful lake of Columbo. It is divided into basons by projecting points, and interspersed with islands; its banks are dotted with villas, and fringed with as great a variety of trees as you see in England; it is only where, on some steep bank, the slender betel lifts its graceful trunk, that we are reminded of being in the East Indies.

We left Pointe de Galle on the nineteenth. Our party consisted of ourselves and three friends, one of whom we accompanied from Bombay, and the other two, Mr and Mrs ——, are inhabitants of Columbo, upon whom the Maha Modeliar always attends on their journeys; and the whole road from Pointe de Galle to Columbo was decorated in the same manner as the rest-houses. The dressing the road for persons of consequence in the government, is a tribute from the fishermen of this coast, and so is the providing lights at night in the manner described in coming from Bellegam. Under the Dutch government, the inhabitants of the villages were required to furnish provisions, and koolis to carry both the palankeens and baggage of travellers without hire; but the English pay punctually for every thing of this kind. The dressing the road and rest-houses, as it is seldom required, and is performed chiefly by the women and children, is no heavy burden, and is merely exacted as a mark of respect to the officers of government. Our first stage was from Pointe de Galle to Heccadua, a considerable village, near which there is a broad river, which we crossed on a stage erected on three small boats, with a canopy of white cotton ornamented with leaves and flowers. We spent the heat of the day under the shade of the young coco-nut wood on the beach at Heccadua. In the afternoon we proceeded to Ambolamgodda, and stopped about half a mile from it to look at a magnificent lake, formed by a large river which descends from the Candian country. The Candians frequently come down this river to barter betel-nut, rice, and precious stones, for salt and some other necessaries,—a traffic that no jealousy of their government can prevent, for, as the English possess the whole of the coast of Ceylon, they have no salt but what they obtain in this manner. There is a long wooden bridge over the stream between the lake and the sea, on which we were met by all the dancing men and musical instruments of the village, to which they conducted us dancing and playing before us all the way. At the entrance of Ambolamgodda we found what I suppose is the militia of the place drawn up to receive us. Three or four old bayonets stuck upon sticks, as many old bear-spears, old pikes, and weapons without names, composed the ragged armour of the ragged crew; and a Madras bed-cover, fluttering on a pole, served for a standard. At the head of this band marched the village Modeliar, who led us to the rest-house, where, after dressing ourselves, we sat down to an excellent dinner of the fish of the coast, part of a wild hog, of which there are great numbers in the island, and other good things; but as I do not mean to record our daily bill of fare, I shall mention at once all the provisions that may be had without going out of Ceylon. The coast abounds with a variety of good fish; domestic quadrupeds require feeding at great expense, owing to the scarcity of fodder, but the poultry is excellent, and the woods occasionally furnish wild hogs, venison, and jungle fowl, besides wild ducks and teal. The fruits are the best I have seen in India of their kind; they are, the pine-apple, the pamplemousse or shaddock, the plantain, and the orange. The coco-nuts are remarkably good, particularly a large kind of a golden colour, called the Rajah's coco-nut. The common people eat great quantities of the Jack-fruit, which they slice and curry while unripe; I, of course, prefer them ripe, but they require to be nicely prepared and steeped in salt water, for the eatable part, when ripe, is bedded in a slimy substance, the smell of which is intolerable. The bread here is extremely good, and the butter made in private houses is only inferior to that in England. The supply of vegetables is very scanty; potatoes and onions are imported from Bombay; and sometimes, but very rarely, cabbage and peas are brought from Bengal.

When I went to my room at night, I found a lamp, of probably a more ancient form than any antique; a solid lump of wood, with a long stick inserted into it, supported half a coco-nut shell, which contained the oil and the wick. The hand of art only was wanting to convert this rude lamp into an elegant piece of furniture; for the log was an unplaned piece of ebony, the stick a fresh bamboo, and the shell itself, whose form as a lamp is beautiful, takes a fine polish.

The next morning after breakfast we went to Cossgodda, a small village, the only stage where we were not on the sea-shore. As we went through the wood, I saw one of the large baboons, called here Wanderows, on the top of a coco-nut tree, where he was gathering nuts, with which he run along the tops of the trees with surprising agility. I at first took him for a man, but I discovered my mistake when he peeped at my palankeen through the leaves, by the large grey ruff he has round his face. From Cossgodda we proceeded to Bentot, where there are the remains of a Dutch fort and town. It is on the side of a very beautiful river, which we crossed in the same manner as we did that near Heccadua. Before breakfast the next morning, Captain ——— and I walked round the neighbouring fields, and were delighted with the beauty of the scenery. There is a little promontory jutting out into the sea, covered with flowers and shrubs, and charmingly shaded; there we sat and watched two small vessels as they sailed at a distance, while the murmurs of the ocean were but now and then hushed enough to allow us to hear the songs of the fishermen on the beach. I cannot sometimes help comparing the different ways in which the same objects affect minds accustomed to different trains of association. The low rocks on the shore, which cause a continual boiling of the water round them, and the stupendous clouds that roll over the main, changing its hue to every various tint as they roll, I have always admired as among the most interesting circumstances of a sea-view; but my companion, though fully sensible of their beauty, feels at the sight of these objects the secret horror that the forerunners of storms and shipwrecks are calculated to inspire.

We left Bentot after breakfast, and arrived at Barbareen about two o'clock, where we found that the provident Modeliar had erected a beautiful rest-house for us, and had prepared an excellent collation. There is a bold projecting rock, nearly insulated, on the top of which is a Mussulman saint's tomb,—a mean little building, overshadowed by four or five coco-nut trees; here the Modeliar had built our bungalo of bamboos, covered with cotton cloth, and decorated with leaves, flowers, and bunches of coco-nuts by way of capitals to the pillars; and across the chasm which separates it from the village, a temporary bridge was thrown, covered with cotton, and decorated like the bungalo. At the foot of the promontory the fishermen sometimes lay up their boats and spread their nets; and the whole scene was so picturesque that I made a sketch of it, after which I joined the party in the rest-house, and enjoyed the freshness of the breeze, which ruffled the open sea, but left the inner bay smooth and clear as a mirror.

Barbareen is a Mussulman village, and the Modeliar is also a Mussulman; the inhabitants are chiefly artizans, who work in

M. G. del.

Publish'd by A. Constable & C° Edinburgh July 1812.

Etch'd by James Storer.

Temporary Bridge & Bungalo at Barbareen

all kinds of metals; we saw several swords and dirks, with their scabbards, of very good workmanship. The next stage to Barbareen is Caltura, where there is an old Dutch fort, commanding a most beautiful view. A broad river flows from the eastern forests, which extend almost as far as the eye can reach, where they are lost, together with the distant mountains, in the horizon. Westward the river empties itself into the ocean, amidst rocks and groves, where the fishermen shelter their boats and build their huts. As I was attempting to sketch the scene, a violent storm of rain, thunder, and lightning came on, with all the grand circumstances peculiar to tropical climates, and forced us to take shelter in the rest-house, where we remained till the next morning, when we crossed the river before day-break. First our palankeens and servants went over in two or three small boats lashed together, and with them a number of people carrying lights; then all the village musicians in separate boats, having also their lights; and lastly our boat, dressed with white cotton, flowers, and leaves, and illuminated with the dried coco-nut leaves. I really never saw so gay a scene; and it was with no small regret that I reached the opposite shore, to shut myself up in my palankeen, and to listen to the monotonous song of my palankeen-bearers.

After breakfasting in a small bungalo on the sea-shore, we reached our friend's house on the lake of Columbo, about two o'clock, and were well pleased to find ourselves settled quietly in a comfortable bungalo, after spending so long a time in wandering, the last four days of which were passed either in travelling in a palankeen, or in a rest-house preparing for it. The distance from Pointe de Galle to Columbo is only seventy-two miles, and might be accomplished in little more than twenty-four hours;

but it is fatiguing to travel so fast, and is attended with considerable expense, as in that case you must have more than double the number of bearers for your palankeen.

March 1.—We have now been at Columbo some days; and I am so delighted with the place, and with the English society here, that if I could choose my place of residence for the rest of the time of my absence from England, it should be Columbo. We generally drive out before breakfast in a bandy, and go sometimes through the fort, which is extremely pretty. It is immediately between the sea and the lake, and only joined to the main-land by a causeway on each side of the water; and sometimes we go through the cinnamon gardens, which lie at the opposite end of the lake. The cinnamon is naturally a tall shrub, or rather tree, but it is kept low in the gardens for the sake of the young bark, which is gathered at two different seasons, though the same plants are not cut every season. When the sticks are cut, the bark is taken off with a little instrument, which peels the whole at once; it is then laid in the sun to dry, when it rolls of itself in the manner in which we see it in the shops. Great nicety is required in laying together a sufficient number of pieces for one roll, and in sorting the different qualities, the finest spice being always at the extremity of the branch. The soil in the gardens is fine white sand. Besides the cinnamon, I saw there the cashew-nut, two kinds of datura, the ixora, and a variety of plants with the names and properties of which I am not acquainted.

A few days ago we joined a large party in an excursion to the governor's country-house, Mount Lavinia. It is a charming residence; it literally overhangs the sea, and has all the beauty that hill and valley, wood and rocks, with a beautiful beach and a fine open sea, can give. The interior, though not large, is very pleasant; a long gallery looks towards the sea; the rooms on the other side command some pretty hills, the sides of which form fine lawns; and in the valley are palm-trees, which hide all the farm-offices, and afford shelter to a collection of animals of the deer and elk kind, from the interior of the island, and from the opposite coast of India. Feeding by himself, we remarked an animal not less beautiful than terrible, the wild bull, whose milk-white hide is adorned with a black flowing mane.

Here I saw specimens of several beautiful kinds of wood in the furniture of the house. The jack-wood, which, at first yellow, becomes on exposure to the air of the colour of mahogany, and is of as fine a grain; the toon, or country mahogany, which comes from Bengal; the ebony, whose black vies with the native jet of the island; the satin-wood, with its silky lustre; the calaminda, whose dark and light veins alternately shew each other to the greatest advantage; and some others of more ordinary appearance, and in more common use.

March 9.—We have been highly gratified by an excursion to Negumbo, whence we went into the jungle to see the manner of taking elephants. We left Columbo early on the sixth; and after breakfasting in a pretty bungalo on the way, we reached Negumbo to dinner, where we were joined by the collector of the district, a learned and ingenious man, and Mr Daniel the painter, whose printed views of Ceylon you must have seen.

Negumbo has a ruinous fort situated on the sea-shore near a small lake. Like most of the old towns in Ceylon, it is very picturesque, being interspersed with trees and fruit-gardens. We slept in the rest-house; and next morning early we set off for the elephant *craal*, or trap, which is sixteen miles from Negumbo, and within half a mile of the Candian frontier. The first eight miles the bandies conveyed us over very good roads; but the marshy ground we had to pass afterwards, obliged us to get into our palankeens, which had been sent on to await us near a talipot tree we wished to see. The talipot is a species of palm like the palmyra, when not in blossom; but when it is crowned with its flower, it is the most magnificent of vegetables. From the centre of its bushy head rises a stem of twelve or fifteen feet, which puts out on every side a number of small branches, covered with a delicate straw-coloured flower, having the appearance of one grand blossom on the top of the tall palm, whose graceful stem, like a pillar crowned with fan-like leaves, form the most beautiful support for its elegant superstructure.

When we reached the craal it was near ten o'clock, and we found the collector and Mr Daniel awaiting us in the breakfast bungalo, where the attention of the former had literally spread a feast in the wilderness. The craal is in the shape of a funnel, the wide part of which extends several hundred feet into the forest, leaving the trees within standing. It is composed of strong posts made of whole trunks of trees driven well into the ground, and lashed to others, placed horizontally, with strong coier ropes. To defend this wall from the fury of the elephants, small fires are lighted near it on the outside, which intimidate the animals so that they do not approach it. The trap is divided into three parts, the outer one of which is only inclosed on three sides, and communicates with the next by a gate made of strong poles, fastened together by ropes so as to permit it to roll up. When the elephants are once driven into the outer chamber, they are prevented from retreating by men stationed at the entrance with different kinds of weapons, but chiefly sticks, on the ends of which are bundles of lighted straw. When a sufficient number are thus collected in the outer inclosure, the hunters close in upon them, and drive them by their shouts and weapons into the second chamber, the gate of which is immediately let down, and they are there confined till it is convenient to take them out. When every thing is prepared for that purpose, the animals are driven into the third and last inclosure, which is also the smallest. One end of it terminates in a long passage, just wide enough for a single beast; and the moment one of them enters it, the hunters thrust strong poles through the interstices in the walls of the craal, and close him in so that he cannot move backwards or forwards. Two tame elephants are then stationed one at each side of the outlet, and putting in their trunks, they hold that of their wild brother till the hunters have passed several bands of rope round his neck, and fastened nooses to each of his feet. A rope is then passed through his neck bands and those of the tame animals; the stakes in front are gradually removed; the ropes drawn tighter; and the prisoner is led out between his two guards, who press him with their whole weight, and thus lead him to the tree or the stake where he is to be fastened. If he be refractory, they beat him with their trunks till he submits; he is sometimes tied by one leg, sometimes by two; if he be very strong and furious, he is fastened by the neck and by all his limbs. I never saw grief and indignation so passionately expressed as by one of these creatures; he groaned, tried to tear his legs from their fetters, buried his trunk in the earth, and threw dust into the air. Not even the choicest food, the plantain tree, or the leaf of the young palm, could tempt him to eat or to forget his captivity for several hours. It sometimes happens that they starve themselves to death; but a few days generally suffices to calm their fury, and their education is immediately begun.

The elephants here are used for drawing timber out of the jungle, and for other public works; but the greater number of those caught in Ceylon are sold to the continent of India. The elephant-keepers teach their beasts a number of tricks, such as walking upon two legs, taking up people with their trunks, tearing up trees, and picking pins or small coins out of the sand. Yet, tame as they are, they are extremely sensible to injuries. One of those we saw, though habitually gentle and obedient, formerly killed a keeper who had been cruel to him. The number and variety of stories concerning the sagacity of the elephant told by those most in the habit of seeing and observing that animal, if they do not prove the truth of each anecdote, are yet strongly presumptive of his wisdom and docility. I was told by a gentleman, that, not long ago, a considerable body of troops had to cross the Kistna, then much swoln by the rains, in doing which, one of the artillery-men who was mounted on a gun fell off in the middle of the stream, immediately before the wheel of the gun-carriage; his comrades gave him up for lost; but an elephant attending on the artillery had seen him fall, and putting his trunk to the wheel, raised it so as to prevent its crushing the man, and then lifted him out of the water unhurt.

After seeing the process of taking the elephants we walked about the jungle till our palankeen boys were sufficiently rested to carry us back to Negumbo, and amused ourselves with the gambols of swarms of red monkeys that were playing in the trees over our heads, and who seemed highly delighted with their unusual company. I saw in the forest innumerable trees and plants which were new to me, among which I was delighted to find the pitcher-plant, Nepenthes distillatoria, or, as it is here called, the monkey-cup. It creeps along the ground, and is mostly found in sandy soils; the flower grows in a spike, and is as little attractive in its appearance as the common dock. The horn or cup grows at the end of the leaf, from which it is separated by a tendril of five or six inches long; it contains, when full, about two gills of water of an excellent pure taste: whether it is dew, or a secretion from the plant, I do not know. A circular cover to the cup flies open when it is nearly at its full growth, and shuts again when it is filled with water. The country people say that, when the monkeys are in want of water, they seek for this plant and drink its contents. I imagine this to be the plant which Campbell, on the authority of Chateaubriant, introduces in his charming poem of Gertrude, as the "lotus-horn;" but it has no resemblance either to the sacred lotus of the east, or to the numerous tribe of lotuses whose flowers are papilionaceous. All the kinds of cane, from the lofty bamboo to the creeping ratan, adorn these forests; the pepper twines round every tree; and the thick underwood is composed of flowering shrubs and gaudy parasite and creeping plants. As we were walking about, we found that the ground was covered with leeches, which stuck to the bare legs of the natives, and which we only kept off by great caution. Unless you choose to submit to a regular bleeding when they have once fastened themselves, you run the risk of getting disagreeable sores in taking them off. They are striped brown and yellow, and have a very wide mouth; they answer the same purposes as the common leeches in England.

The moment our palankeens were ready we began our journey to Negumbo, fearing that we should scarcely get through the jungle before sunset, the night air in the woods occasioning intermittent fevers. We however left Mr Daniel at the craal, where he intended to stay some time in search of subjects for his pencil. To defend himself from the bad effects of his sylvan life, he smokes, and lights great fires within and without his tent. On our road I saw the curious spectacle of an extensive burned forest. Many of the massy trunks had fallen down, and, by stopping the water from running off after the rains, had formed little swamps, where aquatic plants and moss had begun to grow, but the greater part were erect, bare, and bleached, with here and there a creeping plant beginning to grace their barrenness with a foreign verdure.

We returned yesterday to Columbo, and find with regret that we must leave it on our return to Bombay to-morrow. The coast of Ceylon is generally extremely healthy, but none of our troops have been able to stand the noxious effects of a campaign in the jungle. The natives are subject to leprosy and other cutaneous diseases, and I saw many persons afflicted with the Cochin leg or Elephantiasis; the patients walk about apparently without pain for several years, with their legs swoln to the size of their bodies, and the skin stretched and shining; but they often die in great agony at last.

The Cingalese are ingenious workmen in gold and silver; their more useful manufactures are, hemp and coier rope, coarse cotton cloths for domestic consumption, ratan mats and baskets, and cane-work of all kinds. The products of the island, besides timber, elephants, and cinnamon, are hemp, coier, coco-nuts, arrack, precious stones, pearls, and drugs; among which are, Columbo-root, gamboge, and the Datura fastuosa, which the natives use as a cure for the spasmodic asthma, by cutting the root in small pieces, and smoking it like tobacco; the Datura metel, which is most plentiful about Columbo, is said to possess the same qualities.

On board the H. C. Cruiser, Prince of Wales, March 12, *off the Malabar Coast.*—As this is the season when the land and sea breezes become less constant, previous to the setting in of the northerly winds, we are creeping slowly along the coast, and so close to it that we see perfectly well the situation of every place as we pass. Cape Comorin, and the islands in its neighbourhood, make, from sea, like a high rocky point, and from thence the mountains rise as we advance towards the north. In some places they are so near the shore, that they literally seem to overhang it; in others they recede a few miles, leaving space for towns, villages, and fields. They are almost clothed to the top with "majestic woods of every vigorous green;" and it is only here and there that a wide tract of jungle-grass, or a projecting rock, interrupts the deep hue of these ancient forests. At the foot of the ghauts, the white churches of the Christians of St John's and of the Portuguese, appear now and then among the coco-nut woods which fringe the coast, and mix agreeably with the fishermen's huts, the native pagodas, and the ruined forts of decayed European settlements. The night scenery is not less beautiful; it is the custom to burn the jungle-grass before the rains, in order to fertilize the soil; and though the smoke only is visible in the day, at night you see miles of country glowing with red embers, or blazing with vivid flame.

March 18.—Our breezes continue to decrease, and we are consequently obliged to economise our books, that we may make them last till our arrival at Bombay. Our cabin being small and close, we have screens on deck where we spend the day. Our breakfast hour is nine o'clock, after which some one of the party reads aloud till twelve, when we play an hour at whist or backgammon. I then study till half past two, when we dress for dinner. The evening is spent in reading and walking as much as the short quarter-deck of our vessel will allow, and after sunset in conversation. Yesterday our captain, an old seaman, who has been many years in the Company's service, and who has been in every port from the Bocca Tigris in China to the extremities of the Red Sea, was giving us an account of some Indian government expedition, and, endeavouring to fix the date, he said, " Aye, that must have been when we lay in *the river*." I, thinking naturally of the Thames, exclaimed, ' I thought you ' were then in India.'—" Well, so I was."—' What river do you ' mean, then?'—" Why, the Tigris, Bussora river, to be sure." Now, to hear " far Tigris and Balsorah's haven," spoken of with such familiarity by such a man, so completely disenchanted them, and took off the kind of religious respect one acquires for places far off, especially when consecrated by history or fable, that I felt as if the places themselves had been annihilated when the illusions connected with them were destroyed. I should be curious to try if places immortalised by heroic deeds, and the abode of science and philosophy, could thus become uninteresting by a nearer inspection; whether, when the erugo is brushed from the medal, it becomes a common shilling. Surely the plains of Marathon, the Portico and Academy, Pireus and Salamis, could not, on the most intimate acquaintance with their present state and their modern inhabitants, degenerate into common fields, schools, and fishing-towns! But I forget that I am only familiarized with places famed in oriental story, celebrated indeed for conquests and for magnificence, for luxury and for superstition, but not illustrated by virtue or by patriotism. The sacredness of the shades with which the imagination so readily peoples the banks of the Tiber and the Ilyssus, must surely preserve the holiness of their aspect uncontaminated by modern associations, and leave the soul at liberty to follow the visions of heroism, of virtue, of philosophy, which the scenes once inhabited by heroes and sages are calculated to excite.

March 20, *off Calicut.*—We spent the afternoon of yesterday ashore at Calicut, where we busied our imaginations, endeavouring to trace the scenes of the first landing of Europeans in India, the meeting of the Zamorim and Vasco de Gama, the treachery of the prince, and the bravery and presence of mind of the admiral; but the place has passed so often through the hands of conquerors, that every trace of former grandeur and importance is swept away. About four miles north of Calicut is a creek, where some have conjectured that the town of Calicut formerly stood, and where the Portuguese fleet must have lain during the monsoon. There are a few heaps of stones and old walls near the spot; but if it be really the scite of old Calicut, the creek must have been much deeper than it now is, before it could have admitted even one of the ships.

We had no time to visit any thing but the town, as it now stands. In its neighbourhood there are the remains of extensive brick walls, and an old gateway, now overgrown with shrubs. The bazar is extensive, but looks ruinous, owing to the precaution taken here against fire, which is, to uncover all the houses during the dry season, so that nothing but the rafters are left. This custom must frequently expose the inhabitants to great inconvenience, as storms frequently come down with violence from the mountains, as was the case the night we were ashore. About eight o'clock, tremendous thunder and lightning came on, with a deluge of rain which lasted the whole night, and from which not one of the natives had a shelter for himself or his children.

The next morning we walked a few miles into the country to see an English gentleman's house, situated in the bosom of the ghauts. We wandered

> "Through palmy shades and aromatic woods,
> That grace the plains, invest the peopled hills,
> And up the more than Alpine mountains wave."

On our way we saw one of the Zamorim's houses; but he was absent at a more favoured residence at Paniany, a few miles to the south of Calicut, where there is a river sufficiently large, during the rains, to float the timber from the mountain-forests to the sea-shore, and where, in consequence, the government timber-vessels are stationed. Near Calicut we saw the walls of a Nyar's house. These people were the nobles of Malabar, whose brave and turbulent spirit gave so much trouble, not only to the first Portuguese settlers, but to their own sovereigns. Each Nyar's house was a castle surrounded by a bank or wall, and all ingress and egress was by a ladder, drawn up when not in immediate use. But the spirit of the Nyars is broken; and though the wall is still built round the habitation, the ladder is left standing day and night, and of their former fame nothing remains but the reputed beauty of their women.

In our walk we only saw two pagodas, and these are in ruins; worship is however performed in the only remaining apartment of one of them, which is covered with cadjan. These ruins are monuments of Hyder and Tippoo Sultan, the latter of whom caused beef broth to be poured down the throats of several thousand Bramins of this coast, who thus lost their caste, and all the possessions they enjoyed as ministers of the gods,—an involuntary loss of caste being attended with the same fatal consequences as if it were incurred by the commission of a crime. A number of these poor creatures were starved to death, and many put an end to an existence, rendered miserable by the privation of their privileges and dignities.

May 4.—After passing slowly by Telichery, the Anjedive islands, and the picturesque point of Cape Ramas, we came in sight of the fortress of Aguada, at the entrance of the harbour of Goa, and I entertained hopes of landing the next morning to see the old city, with its marble churches and magnificent monasteries, and to pay my respects to the tomb of St Francis Xavier; but a contrary breeze sprung up in the night, and blew us far from the shore, so that I was obliged to reconcile myself to the disappointment, by reflecting on the present misery of that once flourishing colony, which would have embittered any pleasure I could hope for in admiring its exterior beauties. The old town is so unhealthy that a new one has been built at some distance, and the unpeopled streets of the ancient city echo only to the unfrequent tread of some religious procession. The colony is almost abandoned by the mother-country, and its inhabitants scarcely speak their native tongue intelligibly. Their poverty is such, that the women of the best families earn their subsistence by making lace, or artificial flowers, and working muslin.

We are now within sight of the light-house of Bombay, a handsome building on a point of land running south-west from the island, called Colaba, or Old Woman's Island; the passage between it and Bombay is fordable at low water. To the south of the harbour's mouth are the two small islands of Henery and Kenery: the anchoring ground is between Butcher's Island and Bombay fort; but there is a fine bay above Elephanta, where the Portuguese used to lay up their fleet during the monsoon, and which is nearly land-locked.

Bhandoop, Island of Salsette, May 20, 1810.—I am glad to find myself in a quiet country residence, free from the noise and the clouds of dust of Bombay. I cannot better describe the country of Salsette than by the following extract of a letter from the friend with whom I am now living; it was written during the rainy season, so that some of the finest features are now deficient. "The hills were already covered with verdure, except near the "tops, which, still black and bare, exhibited a striking and a- "greeable contrast. The torrents were rapid and large, and "their roaring, as they fell down the sides of the precipices at a "great distance, mixed with the rustling of the palms, was grand, "and gave me a clearer idea of the circumstances of a moun- "tainous country than I ever had before. The travelling home "through the more cultivated part of Salsette, the green and "exquisitely beautiful paysage, transported me in imagination to "happier countries. In one situation, an old bridge of seven "arches, constructed by the Portuguese, and appearing in an "oblique direction across the landscape, with a ruined tower in "its neighbourhood, a fine rapid stream passing under it, the "most luxuriant tamarind and mango trees hanging over its ex-

" tremities, and bandaries driving their cattle in the fore-ground, " recalled to my mind the pictures of Claude Lorraine."

Bhandoop is about twenty miles from Bombay, and six from Tannah, the capital of Salsette. The country round it is beautiful; but I scarcely walk out without seeing some traces of the devastations caused by war, and perpetuated by a narrow policy. It is grievous to see whole tracts, once cultivated by the Portuguese, utterly abandoned, and covered with jungle. On the sides of many of the hills may be traced terraces one above another, raised to facilitate cultivation, now gone to ruin, and the vines they supported run wild; and though the fruit forms, it never comes to maturity.

Salsette now scarcely produces a hundredth part of what it might supply, and it is in proportion thinly inhabited. I have heard several native merchants in Bombay say, that if the government would let the uncultivated lands at such a rent as might not be grievous to the occupier, while bringing it into cultivation, or even if the taxes were subject to the same regulations as in Bombay, they would be glad to farm large portions of the island; but that at present, Salsette being subject to the method of taxation used by the Mahrattas, and the anxiety of the government to get a high present rent for its farms, blinding it to the future advantages to be derived from the encouragement of husbandry, the rents are so excessive that they are afraid to undertake any improvements of the soil.

My friend Mr A. inherited a considerable estate in Salsette, which he lets to native cultivators on easy terms, and is at the expense of making wells, absolutely necessary for all kinds of crops, as the ground requires constant irrigation, and many kinds of grain must be flooded for some weeks, leaving several inches of water upon the surface. The lands are thus easily brought into cultivation; and Mr A.'s tenants find an immediate market at his distillery of Bhandoop, where an immense quantity of spirits of different kinds is made. Besides the sugar-cane and rice, the immediate produce of Salsette, dates from Arabia, and other fruits, with tary of every kind of palm-tree, are used in the distillery. The work is usually stopped in the hot season, as the evaporation takes place so slowly at that time, that the operation is carried on at great loss. I found the overseer, a sensible Chinese, busy at the door of the distillery writing his daily accounts, which he first calculated, with astonishing quickness, by means of a square frame, crossed by wires, on which are strung moveable balls. His writing materials are the common Indian or Chinese ink, which we use for drawing, and fine hair pencils. The Chinese paper is extremely brittle, and the best is composed of two or more sheets pasted together, pressed and glazed. On the overseer's table stood a tea-pot and cup, with cold strong tea, and he shewed me a packet of clothes and eatable delicacies he had just received from Canton; the former consisted only of loose trowsers, long jackets, and shoes of various stuffs. As the weather grows warmer or colder, a Chinese increases or diminishes the number of his coats, so that I have seen them sometimes with only one, and sometimes with nine or ten. The eatables consisted of dried sharks fins, birds nests, and a variety of gelatinous sea-weeds, none of which appeared at all inviting.

But as I wish to remark all that is uncommon in my travels, I must not omit the character of my hostess, if indeed I can do justice to it. I have seen women in India pretend that, on account of the climate, they were too sickly to nurse their own children, too weak to walk in their own gardens, too delicate to approach a native hut, lest they should be shocked by the sight of poverty or sickness. But Mrs A. with the face and the heart of an angel, is received like one by the poor and the wretched. I have followed her in admiration through a village where her appearance made every face to smile. She is blessed alike by the old and the young; she knows all their wants, and listens to all their complaints. There is no medical man within many miles, and I have seen her lovely hands binding up wounds which would have sickened an ordinary beholder. The work of charity over, she enjoys a walk amidst these beautiful scenes with all the gaiety natural to her age. She says, " Qui fait aimer les champs, fait " aimer la vertu;" and one of her chief pleasures lies in the contemplation of the beauties of nature. Her family consists of the daughter of a friend, whom she instructs with the diligence of a mother, a little black boy whom she rescued from famine, and whom she is bringing up as a mechanic, and her own two infants. Mrs A.'s accomplishments are above those of most women. Her drawing is that of an artist, and her delineations of the costume of the natives are beautiful; her judgment in music is exquisite, and her taste correct in both ancient and modern literature. Her language is pure and elegant; her voice in speaking is charming, and her manner is gentle and unembarrassed. She puts me in mind of those gems which bear the highest relief and the deepest intaglio, and that yet take the brightest polish. Would that there were a few more such European women in the East, to redeem the character of our country-women, and to shew the Hindoos what English Christian women are.

Toulsi, May 24, 1810.—I came here yesterday with Dr and Mrs S. who are encamped near the village of Toulsi, for the convenience of visiting the caves of Canary, which were about two miles off. Mrs S. is a very pretty and highly accomplished woman, who has travelled a good deal in India, and possesses a considerable share of information on most subjects relating to this country.

The landscape all around us is grandly wild, and increases in boldness on approaching the caverns, where we went yesterday. The first that we came to resembles that of Carli in the interior, but it does not appear to have been so highly finished. Besides, the Portuguese having formerly fitted it up as a church, thought it no doubt incumbent on them to deface the most pagan looking parts. The fine teak ribs for supporting the roof, are almost all gone; but the holes in the rock for receiving them, still mark where they have been. The portico is not near so fine as that at Carli; but there are some not inelegant figures. On the two sides are two gigantic statues of twenty-five feet high, standing erect, with their hands hanging close to the body, and the heels close together. They resemble extremely the figures of Bhud I saw in Ceylon, only that, instead of the flame-like ornament on the top of his head, there is a cushion of the same curly appearance with the rest of the hair. The rough screen in front of the cave is like that of Carli, but is in better preservation; before it are two pillars attached to the rock, one finished with a capital of grotesque figures, and the other plain. About fourteen paces from the screen are the remains of a low highly ornamented rocky fence. On each side of the great cave there are smaller ones, apparently unfinished. That on the right hand is occupied by one of the solid temples I mentioned, as occupying the circular end of the Carli cave; and there is also one in the same situation in the great cave here. Leaving this groupe of caves, we ascend-

M. G. del. Etch'd by James Storr

Entrance to the Great Cave at Kenary.

Pub^d by A. Constable & Co. Edinburgh June 1. 1812.

ed the hill by a very rude path, which leads to steps cut in the rock; and found not a few caves, as I expected, but a whole city excavated in the mountain, which is perfectly bare, but surrounded by woody hills. Some of the caves are small, and seem adapted for private dwellings; to each of these there is a reservoir of excellent water; others are large, and I could imagine them the residence of priests or persons of distinction. One in particular has a long viranda in front; the chamber within is about forty feet square, its sides are covered with figures of Jine saints, four of which are standing, the others sitting in the posture of meditation, or reasoning, with the fore-finger of the right hand applied to the thumb of the left. Narrow door-ways in three sides of the cave lead to cells of ten feet by six, in each of which there is a raised seat; the fourth side has one door, and several windows looking into the viranda. The small caves are in a variety of shapes, and the pillars that support them are not less various; yet I think none of them are ugly, and many are very elegant, The large square cave is in a ravine, where there are shrubs and trees; over it the stones dug from other caves are piled, so as to support earth, where a few trees flourish, and render the spot cooler than any other part of this subterraneous city; for, excepting here, there is no vegetation but now and then an euphorbia, which seems to root in the stone itself. The top of the mountain commands a fine prospect over woods and mountains, and arms of the sea, to the continent of India on the one hand, and to the ocean on the other. Here are reservoirs of excellent water, and baths dug in the rock, the access to which, as well as the communication between the caves, is facilitated by flights of steps cut in the mountain. The caves of Canary, like that of Carli, contain inscriptions in an unknown character. At Ambola, a mountain at the west end of Salsette, there are some caverns of the same appearance as that of Elephanta, and decorated, like it, with figures referable to the Brahminical superstitions; but I fear I shall not have time to visit them this year.

Bhandoop, May 28.—I left Toulsi the day after our expedition to the caves, in time to reach Bhandoop by day-light, as the tigers in the hills are so numerous as to render travelling after sunset very dangerous. The following afternoon an additional party of friends arrived from Bombay, and I accompanied them to Caliane. We slept at Doncala, a country house belonging to the judge of the district, and the next morning we got into a pleasure-boat at Tannah to proceed to Caliane. The river, or rather arm of the sea, at that place, is very narrow, I should think hardly more than a furlong across; the fort is upon the beach, and on the opposite side are the rocks and hills of the Mahrattas, with houses and meadows below them close to the water's edge. The morning was delightful, but the breeze gradually died away, and it became the hottest day I ever experienced. Our rowers exerted themselves to reach Caliane before the tide should turn, and we accordingly got there about one o'clock. One of our party had an idea that we might discover some ruin or vestige of Grecian antiquity at this place, as many authors affirm that the Greeks, the Egyptians, and the Romans, traded with this port, formerly a considerable city, though now a poor Mussulman town. We landed in high spirits, determined to see antique Greece at every turn; but after a fatiguing walk of two hours in the burning sun, we gave up the search as fruitless. I believe the natives thought us mad, when we told them we wished to see old houses and broken walls, of which they shewed us plenty, but not one of the kind of which we were in search. Indeed, if any such ever existed, the numerous sieges sustained by the town from the Mahomedans and from the Mahrattas, must long since have swept them away. It is only lately that Caliane has ceased to be a place of considerable trade; it is still a populous town, and carries on some traffic in coco-nuts, oil, coarse cloths, brass, and earthen ware.

Disappointed in the objects of our search ashore, we would have got into the boat, and taken what refreshment we had brought with us; but here the tide was against us, the bar was dry, and we had to wait under a banian tree for three hours before the boat could float. On examining our provisions, we had the mortification to discover that the sun had spoiled one half of them, and on the rest we were now obliged to make our dinner, and, as it turned out, our supper also. However, the good humour of the party got the better of their misfortunes; but repeated repartee is always stupid, and to you, in the midst of the wits of our Scotish Athens, jokes from the Mahratta country must be dull indeed!

At five o'clock we got into our bark; but at the bar, half a mile from Caliane, were obliged to get out to lighten her, and walked down the banks of the river through a wood, where we found great quantities of the corinda berry, which in taste resembles a fine plumb, but in size and appearance is like the berry of the laurel, to which the whole plant has a great resemblance. About sunset we were again able to embark, but we got aground four times on different ledges of rock. Meantime the sky began to lower, large drops of rain fell, and about ten o'clock vivid flashes of lightning ushered in the first monsoon squall. The wind, the rain, and the thunder, soon put an end to the exertions of the rowers, and for the next two hours they lay under their benches, excepting when, by the boat's drifting on the rocks, they were obliged to jump overboard to shove her off. By this time the rain had made its way through the roof of our cabin; we were in utter darkness but for the flashing of the lightning, and heard no sound but that of the storm, or, when it lulled, the roaring of the wild beasts. From this disagreeable situation we were relieved by a calm, which enabled the boatmen to reach Tannah at one o'clock, where we were glad to find our palankeens, and, in spite of the fear of tigers, my hamauls brought me to Bhandoop in an hour, fully resolving never again to undertake an expedition by water at the beginning of the monsoon.

Trincomale, June 20, 1810.—Once more I find myself in Ceylon, or, as my great predecessor Sinbad the sailor calls it, Serendib. I left my friends at Bhandoop on the 31st of May, and on the first of June I sailed from Bombay in H. M. ship Illustrious, commanded by Captain Broughton, who accompanied Vancouver in his voyage round the world. We stood out to sea for two days, to look for a favourable wind, as the monsoon was already set in in the neighbourhood of Bombay, and on the twelfth day from our departure we anchored in the Back-bay of Trincomale, a distance of between twelve and thirteen hundred miles. Here we found the commander-in-chief, Admiral Drury, with seven ships of war, so that we seemed almost to have arrived at a British port. The scenery of Trincomale is the most beautiful I ever saw; I can compare it to nothing but Loch Catrine on a gigantic scale. The ships are now lying in Back-bay, but the inner harbour is safe at all seasons; it is so land-locked, that it appears like a lake. Yesterday we rode before breakfast to fort Osnaburg, on a high point of land, commanding both divisions of the inner harbour. The bay, gleaming with the rising sun, seemed like a sheet of liquid gold, broken into creeks and bays, studded with verdant isles, and inclosed by mountains feathered with wood to the summit; while from the nearer crags the purple convolvulus, the white moon-flower, and the scarlet and yellow gloriosa, floated like banners in the wind.

The outer bay is formed by a bold projecting rock, at the extremity of which are the remains of a Hindoo temple. Six pillars, beautifully carved, and supporting a cornice and roof, now form the portico of a British artillery hospital; and a seventh pillar is placed on the summit of a rock opposite. We were told that some caves exist in the neighbourhood, but whether natural or artificial we could not ascertain, neither could we procure a guide to them.

Trincomale was formerly considered very unhealthy, but there does not appear to be any local circumstance to render it so, and the complaints of it on that head are daily decreasing. Like the rest of the coast of Ceylon, the soil had been found unfit for raising vegetables; but, by the exertions of Admiral Drury, a colony of Chinese, similar to that at Pointe de Galle, has established a large garden, whose products are already such as to promise the fairest success. The admiral has also been at pains to import cattle and poultry, and to distribute them among the natives, so as, if possible, to secure a supply for the fleet. Timber is in great plenty, and easy of access, and there are many coves where ships may be hove down with the greatest safety at all seasons; so that repairs can be performed here at less cost than at any other place in India, though the rise of tide is not sufficient at any season for the building of docks.

The first account of Trincomale, as an European settlement, is, that in 1672, De la Haye, a Frenchman, attempted an establishment here, but being opposed by the Dutch governor of Ceylon, Richloff Van Goen, he abandoned it, and went to the coast of Coromandel, and settled at St Thomé, then belonging to the king of Golconda. The Dutch forts now remaining are out of repair; they seem never to have been strong, and the town is small and mean. There are but few European inhabitants, so that the society is composed almost exclusively of the officers of the regiments stationed there. The lower people are chiefly Hindoos from the opposite coast; the only native Cingalese I saw were a few gold and silver smiths, whose chains and other ornaments equal those of Tritchinopoly. The troops now here are divisions of two Malay regiments, and his majesty's 66th regiment, besides a company of artillery. The other day the officers gave a ball and supper to their naval brethren. The colours of the regiment were suspended over the supper table, and the whole was decorated with flowers and branches of trees. In return, parties are constantly going off to the ships; and yesterday we had a grand spectacle; every ship in the bay (among which were two seventy fours and four frigates,) fired two broadsides. I never saw any thing so beautiful as the effect of the clouds of smoke, as they first obscured the whole horizon, and then gradually rolling off, left the ships brightly reflected in the water, which was clear and smooth as a mirror. Nor were the thundering reverberations from the rocks less striking, amidst the grand silence and calmness of nature around.

Madras, July 12, 1810.—When our fleet at Trincomale dispersed, each ship to her station, by the admiral's permission I accompanied Captain Graham in the Hecate to this place, where we arrived on the third day from our departure, the distance being between two and three hundred miles. I do not know any thing more striking than the first approach to Madras. The low flat sandy shore extending for miles to the north and south, for the few hills there are appear far inland, seems to promise nothing but barren nakedness, when, on arriving in the roads, the town and fort are like a vision of enchantment. The beach is crowded with people of all colours, whose busy motions at that distance, make the earth itself seem alive. The public offices and store-houses which line the beach, are fine buildings, with colonnades to the upper stories, supported by rustic bases arched, all of the fine Madras chunam, smooth, hard, and polished as marble. At a short distance Fort-George, with its lines and bastions, the government house and gardens, backed by St Thomas's Mount, form an interesting part of the picture, while here and there in the distance, minarets and pagodas are seen rising from among the gardens.

A friend who, from the beach, had seen our ship coming in, obligingly sent the *accommodation-boat* for us, and I soon discovered its use. While I was observing its structure and its rowers, they suddenly set up a song, as they called it, but I do not know that I ever heard so wild and plaintive a cry. We were getting into the surf; the cockswain now stood up, and with his voice and his foot kept time vehemently, while the men worked their oars backwards, till a violent surf came, struck the boat, and carried it along with a frightful violence; then every oar was plied to prevent the wave from taking us back as it receded, and this was repeated five or six times, the song of the boatmen rising and falling with the waves, till we were dashed high and dry upon the beach. The boats used for crossing the surf are large and light, made of very thin planks sewed together, with straw in the seams, for caulking would make them too stiff; and the great object is, that they should be flexible, and give to the water like leather, otherwise they would be dashed to pieces. Across the very edge of the boat are the bars on which the rowers sit; they are naked all but a turban, and a half handkerchief fastened to the waist by a pack-thread. They are wild-looking, and their appearance is not improved by the crust of salt left upon their bodies by the sea-water, and which generally whitens half their skin. At one end of the boat is a bench with cushions and a curtain, for passengers, so that they are kept dry while the surf is breaking round the boat.

We were hardly ashore when we were surrounded by above a hundred *Dubashis* and servants of all kinds, pushing for employment. The Dubashis undertake to interpret, to buy all you want, to change money, to provide you with servants, tradesmen, and palankeens, and, in short, to do every thing that a stranger finds it irksome to do for himself. We went immediately to our friend's garden-house; for at Madras every body lives in the country, though all offices and counting-houses, public and private, are in the fort or in town. The garden-houses are generally of only one story; they are of a pretty style of architecture, having their porticos and virandas supported by pillars of chunam; the walls are of the same material, either white or coloured, and the floors are covered with ratan mats, so that it is impossible to be more cool. The houses are usually surrounded by a field or *compound*, with a few trees and shrubs, but it is with incredible pains that flowers or fruit are raised. During the hot winds, *tats* (a kind of mat), made of the root of the koosa grass *, which has an agreeable smell, are placed against the doors and windows, and constantly watered, so that as the air blows through them, it spreads an agreeable scent and freshness through the house.

July 16.—I went the other day to see the naval hospital here, a large handsome building, with an excellent garden, and very well appointed. On the top is a large platform, where the convalescents take exercise and enjoy fresh air, with the view over all Madras, its petah or Black-town, and garden-houses, to the shipping in the roads. There is a rope-walk attached to the hospital, but it wants air and is rather short; it however furnishes employment for the invalids. From the hospital I went to see the garden which the late Dr Anderson had planted as a botanical garden, at a vast expense, but it is now in a sad state of ruin. I remarked there the *Saguerus Rumphii*, a kind of palm, from which an excellent kind of sago is made. It is also valuable on account of the black fibres surrounding the trunk at the insertion of the leaves, which afford a cordage for ships, said to be stronger and more durable than that made from any other vegetable substance. I saw also the Nopaul, a kind of prickly pear, on a species of which the cochineal insect lives, and which is now cultivated in Madras as an esculent vegetable. It was brought here merely as a curious exotic, but was discovered by

* *Koosa grass, Poa cynosuroides.* This grass is considered as sacred, and is used in sacrifices. Devotees generally hold it in their hands. In the Hutopodesa there is a story of a tiger who held a blade of koosa grass in order to pass for a holy person, and to conceal his evil and cruel designs.

Dr Anderson to be a valuable antiscorbutic, and has since been used in all men of war on the Indian station, which are now almost free from that dreadful malady the scurvy: The nopaul keeps fresh, and even continues to vegetate long after it is gathered; it makes an excellent pickle, which is now issued to the ships of war.

We had heard so much in Europe of the slight of hand practised by the Madras jugglers, that we were very curious to see some of them. Accordingly we yesterday procured an excellent set to exhibit before us. After shewing the common tricks with the cups and balls, which were changed so as to elude the most narrow observation, and making me start at finding a serpent in my hand when I was sure I received a pebble, the principal exhibitor took up a pinch of white sand between his finger and thumb, and scattering it gently before us, dropped it of a red, blue, or yellow colour, as we required; but that which pleased me most was throwing up eight balls into the air, so as to keep them in a ring at equal distances for a considerable time. He performed a variety of other tricks, in which, being naked from the waist upwards, he could derive no advantage from the concealment of any of his implements in his dress. The small exhibitions being over, the juggler took a round stone, as large as his head, between his heels, and making a spring with it, he threw it to a considerable height, and caught it on his shoulder, whence, by another effort, he threw it and caught it on his back, and so on, receiving it on his sides, the inner part of his elbow, his wrist, or his stomach. But the most curious, though disgusting sight, was the swallowing the sword, and in this there is no deception, for I handled the weapon both before and after he performed the operation. I should have thought that this exercise would have injured him, but he is the healthiest looking native I have seen, well made and proportioned. They begin this trade when very young, the children exercising with short bits of bamboo, which are lengthened as the throat and stomach are able to bear them,—a curious proof of the power of education over the body.

August 1.—I have just returned from a week's excursion to Ennore, a fishing village eight miles north of Madras, where there is a small salt-water lake, with abundance of fine fish and excellent oysters. These attractions have induced a party of gentlemen to build a house by subscription on the edge of the lake, where there is a meeting every week to eat fish, play cards, and sail about on the lake in two little pleasure-boats, a diversion which cannot be enjoyed anywhere else near Madras on account of the surf. We went to Ennore by the canal which is cut from Madras to Pulicat, and met a fleet of thirty-six boats from the latter place laden with charcoal, for the use of the kitchens of Madras. Ennore is a flat sandy place, with about a hundred huts and two European houses, besides the subscription-house. I walked to the beach to see the catamarans of this coast; they are formed of two light logs of wood lashed together, with a small piece inserted between them at one end, to serve as a stem-piece; they are always unlashed, and laid to dry in the sun when they come out of the water, as dryness is essential to their lightness and buoyancy; when ready for the water, they hold two men with their paddles, who launch themselves through the surf to fish, or to carry letters and provisions to ships, when no boat can venture out. These men wear a pointed cap made of matting, in which they secure the papers with which they may be entrusted, though they should themselves be washed off their catamarans a dozen times before they reach the place of their destination. A particular police regulates the catamarans, accommodation-boats, and bar-boats, which last only differ from the accommodation-boats in being smaller and less convenient. Medals are given to such of the boatmen as have saved drowning persons, or have distinguished themselves by fidelity in carrying papers or conveying papers or passengers through the surf in dangerous weather.

August 10.—I have been much pleased with a visit to the female orphan assylum. It seems admirably conducted, and the girls neat, and very expert at all kinds of needle-work. It is really gratifying to see so many poor creatures well brought up, and put in the way of gaining a livelihood. There is likewise a male orphan asylum, where the boys are brought up to different trades. If such establishments are wanted anywhere, it is in India, where the numbers of half-caste, and therefore (if I may use the expression), half-parented children, exceed what one could imagine. I cannot but think it a cruelty to send children of colour to Europe, where their complexion must subject them to perpetual mortification. Here, being in their own country, and associating with those in the same situation with themselves, they have a better chance of being happy.

The language spoken at Madras by the natives is the *Talinga*, here called *Malabars*. The men-servants are all Hindoos, but the women are mostly Portuguese. The palankeen-bearers are called Bhoïs, and are remarkable for strength and swiftness. They have a peculiar song, or cry, with which they amuse themselves on a journey; at first it sounds like the expression of pain and weariness, but it presently breaks out into sounds of exultation.

I have not seen any banians at Madras, but there are a number of hawkers who resemble the borahs. I often see natives of Pondichery, French converts, going about with boxes of lace and artificial flowers, made chiefly by the ladies of the decayed French families in that settlement. There is something in the gaiety of the French character that communicates itsef to all around. I have seen a black man from Pondichery, handle a lace, a flower, a ribbon, with all the air of a fine gentleman, and in his rags shew more politeness and gallantry, than half our Madras civil servants are possessed of. Besides these French pedlars, there are a set of Mahomedans, who go about selling moco stones, petrified tamarind wood, garnets, coral, mock amber*, and a variety of other trinkets, and who are, in their way, as amusing as the Frenchmen. The manner of living among the English at Madras has a great deal more of external elegance than at Bombay; but the same influences operating on the society, I find it neither better nor worse. I am told that it was once more agreeable. I do not wonder that it should have altered, for, during the late unhappy disputes between the government and the army, everybody sided with one party or the other, which of course begot a jealousy still rankling in the minds of all. I am happy that we were not here at the crisis; for though every good citizen must wish, where the civil and military powers come to an open rupture, that the former should prevail, I cannot help feeling that, in this instance, the army was in the outset the injured party, and as some of my

* The petrified tamarind wood is found in the sand near Madras. It takes a beautiful polish, and makes pretty ornaments. The mock amber is the gum of a tree in the Malabar forests, which so much resembles the gum copal that the coachmakers in Bengal use it as a varnish.

friends were of the same way of thinking, I am glad I was not here to countenance, by participating, feelings of which it was so necessary to get the better.

August 18.—I was two evenings ago at a public ball in the Pantheon, which contains, besides a ball-room, a very pretty theatre, card-rooms, and virandas. During the cold season there are monthly assemblies, with occasional balls all the year, which are very well conducted. The Pantheon is a handsome building; it is used as a free-masons lodge of modern masons, among whom almost every man in the army and navy who visits Madras enrols himself. The only other public place at Madras is the Mount Road, leading from Fort-George to St Thomas's Mount. It is smooth as a bowling-green, and planted on each side with banian and yellow tulip trees. About five miles from the fort, on this road, stands a cenotaph to the memory of Lord Cornwallis. It has cost an immense sum of money, but is not remarkable for good taste; however, I love to see public monuments in any shape to great men. It is the fashion for all the gentlemen and ladies of Madras to repair, in their gayest equipages, to the Mount Road, and after driving furiously along, they loiter round and round the cenotaph for an hour, partly for exercise, and partly for the opportunity of flirting and displaying their fine clothes, after which they go home, to meet again every day in the year. But the greatest lounge at Madras is during the visiting hours, from nine o'clock till eleven, when the young men go from house to house to retail the news, ask commissions to town for the ladies, bring a bauble that has been newly set, or one which the lady has obliquely hinted, at a shopping party the day before, she would willingly purchase, but that her husband does not like her to spend so much, and which she thus obtains from some young man, one quarter of whose monthly salary is probably sacrificed to his gallantry. When all the visitors who have any business are gone to their offices, another troop of idlers appears, still more frivolous than the former, and remains till *tiffin*, at two o'clock, when the real dinner is eaten, and wines and strong beer from England are freely drank. The ladies then retire, and for the most part undress, and lye down with a novel in their hands, over which they generally sleep. About five o'clock the master of the family returns from his office; the lady dresses herself for the Mount Road; returns, dresses, dines, and goes from table to bed, unless there be a ball, when she dresses again, and dances all night; and this, I assure you, is a fair, very fair, account of the usual life of a Madras lady.

Calcutta, Sept. 8, 1810.—Business of a most distressing nature requiring my presence at Calcutta, I left Madras, on the 26th of August, in his Majesty's ship Illustrious, and arrived here so late as to make it impossible to return to Madras before the month of December, as the monsoon is set in on the coast; and I have, moreover, missed the friend to whom I came, so I am here a stranger, and in a manner a prisoner. From the time of my embarking the weather was cloudy and hot. After sailing slowly along the low coast, which was constantly obscured by haze, and passing the Jagernauth Pagoda, which stands by itself on a beach of sand, that seems to have no end, the first land we made was Point Palmyras, or rather the tops of the trees which give their name to this low sandy cape. On anchoring in Balasore Roads, the breakers, and the colour of the water, told us that we were in the neighbourhood of land, though none was visible in any direction. The water looked like thick mud, fitter to walk upon than to sail through. Here we left the ship, and proceeded in a pilot's schooner. Nothing can be more desolate than the entrance to the Hoogly. To the west, frightful breakers extend as far as the eye can reach, and you are surrounded by sharks and crocodiles; but on the east is a more horrible object, the black low island of Sangor. The very appearance of the dark jungle that covers it is terrific. You see that it must be a nest of serpents, and a den of tigers; but it is worse, it is the yearly scene of human sacrifice, which not all the vigilance of the British government can prevent. The temple is ruined, but the infatuated votaries of Kali plunge into the waves that separate the island from the Continent, in the spot where the blood-stained fane once stood, and crowned with flowers and robed in scarlet, singing hymns to the goddess, they devote themselves to destruction; and he who reaches the opposite shore without being devoured by the sacred sharks, becomes a pariah, and regards himself as a being detested by the gods. Possessed by this frenzy of superstition, mothers have thrown their infants into the jaws of the sea monsters, and furnished scenes too horrible for description; but the yearly assembly at Sangor is now attended by troops, in order to prevent these horrid practices, so that I believe there are *now* but few involuntary victims. As we advanced up the river, the breakers disappeared, the jungle grew higher and lighter, and we saw sometimes a pagoda, or a village between the trees. The river was covered with boats of every shape, villas adorned the banks, the scene became enchanting, all cultivated, all busy, and we felt that we were approaching a great capital. On landing, I was struck with the general appearance of grandeur in all the buildings; not that any of them are according to the strict rules of art, but groupes of columns, porticoes, domes, and fine gateways, interspersed with trees, and the broad river crowded with shipping, made the whole picture magnificent.

Sept. 16.—On my arrival at Calcutta, I went to the house appointed by the Indian government for captains of the navy, intending to stay there till I procured a lodging to remain in till I could return to Madras; but I had not been many hours on shore, before I received several invitations from the hospitable inhabitants of Calcutta, to live in their houses till I could rejoin my friends. Among the first of these the governor-general, the only person with whom I had been acquainted at home, called, and kindly insisted on my taking up my abode in the government-house, which I did accordingly the next day, when I was introduced to his daughter-in-law and the other ladies of the family. Never was a stranger more kindly received, and never did attentions come in so welcome a time, or in a form so agreeable.

Oct. 22.—The English society of Calcutta, as it is more numerous, affords a greater variety of character, and a greater portion of intellectual refinement, than that of either of the other presidencies. I have met with some persons of both sexes in this place, whose society reminded me of that we have enjoyed together in Britain, when some of the wisest and best of our countrymen, whose benevolence attracted our attention, as their talents commanded our esteem, loved to relax from their serious occupations in the circle of their friends. Among the few here who know and appreciate these things, the most agreeable speculations are always those that point homeward to that Europe, where the mind of man seems to flourish in preference to any other land. If we look round us, the passive submission, the apathy, and the degrading superstition of the Hindoos; the more active fanaticism of the Mussulmans; the avarice, the prodigality, the ignorance, and the vulgarity of most of the white people, seem to place them all on a level, infinitely below that of the least refined nations of Europe.

Oct. 25.—This is the season of festivals; I hear the tomtoms, drums, pipes, and trumpets in every corner of the town, and I see processions in honour of Kali going to a place two miles off, called Kali Ghaut, where there has long been a celebrated temple to this goddess, which is now pulled down, and another more magnificent is to be erected in its place. In all the bazars, at every shop door, wooden figures and human heads, with the neck painted blood-colour, are suspended, referring, I imagine, to the human sacrifices formerly offered to this deity, who was, I believe, the tutelary goddess of Calcutta. Three weeks ago, the festival of Kali, under the name and attributes of Doorga, was celebrated. On this occasion her images, and those of some other divinities, were carried in procession with great pomp, and bathed in the Hoogly, which, being a branch of the Ganges, is sacred. The figures were placed under canopies, which were gilt and decked with the most gaudy colours, and carried upon men's heads. Several of these moving temples went together, preceded by musical instruments, banners, and bare-headed Bramins, repeating *muntras* (forms of prayer). The gods were followed by cars, drawn by oxen or horses, gaily caparisoned, bearing the sacrificial utensils, accompanied by other Bramins, and the procession was closed by an innumerable multitude of people of all castes. This feast lasted several days. I received a printed card on the occasion, which I transcribe:—" Maha Rajah, Rajhissen Bahaudur, " presents his respectful compliments to *Mrs Gram*, and requests " the honour of *his* company to a nautch (being Doorga Poojah), " on the 5th, 6th, and 7th of October, at nine o'clock in the " evening." Having never seen a nautch, I did not decline the Maha Rajah's invitation; but on the evening of the fifth I went, with a small party, to the assembly, and received more amusement than I expected. The Maha Rajah has a fine house at the end of Chitpore bazar. The room into which we were ushered was a large square court, covered in for the occasion with red cloth, to which a profusion of white artificial flowers was fastened. Three sides of the court are occupied by the dwelling-house, the walls of which are adorned by a double row of pillars in couplets, and between each couplet is a window. The fourth side is occupied by the family temple, of a very pretty architecture; the arches which support it are not unlike those used in England in Henry VII.'s time, with cinquefoil heads. A flight of steps leads to the viranda of the temple, where Vishnu sat in state, with a blaze of light before him, in magnificent chandeliers. When we entered there were some hundreds of people assembled, and there seemed to be room for as many more. The dancing was begun, but as soon as our host perceived us he led us to the most commodious seats, stationed boys behind us with round fans of red silk, with gold fringe, and then presented us with bouquets of the mogue and the rose, tied up in a green leaf, ornamented with silver fringe. A small gold vase being brought, the Maha Rajah, with a golden spoon, perfumed us with ottur, and sprinkled us with rose-water, after which we were allowed to sit still and look on. The first dancers were men, whom by their dresses I took for women, though I was rather surprised at the assurance of their gestures, which had nothing else remarkable in them. These gave way to some Cashmerian singers, whose voices were very pleasing. They were accompanied by an old man, whose long white beard and hair, and fair skin, spoke a more northern country than Bengal. His instrument was a peculiarly sweet-toned guitar, which he touched with skill and taste, to some of the odes of Hafiz and some Hindostanee songs. I was sorry when they finished, to make way for a kind of pantomime, in which men personated elephants, bears, and monkeys. After this some women danced; but though they were pretty, and their motions rather graceful, I was disappointed, after hearing so much of the nautch-girls of India. One of them, while dancing in a circle, twisted a piece of striped muslin into flowers, keeping each stripe for a different coloured flower. The last amusement we staid to partake of, was the exhibition of a ventriloquist (the best I ever heard), although the Mahajah pressed us to remain, saying that he had different sets of dancers, enough to exhibit during the whole night. I was pleased with the attention the Rajah paid to his guests, whether Hindoos, Christians, or Mussulmans; there was not one to whom he did not speak kindly, or pay some compliment on their entrance; and he walked round the assembly repeatedly, to see that all were properly accommodated.

I was sorry I could not go to his nautch the next night, where I hear there was a masquerade, when several Portuguese and Pariahs appeared as Europeans, and imitated our dances, music, and manners. I grieve that the distance kept up between the Europeans and the natives, both here and at Madras, is such, that I have not been able to get acquainted with any native families as I did at Bombay. There seems however to be little difference in their manner of living. Their houses appear to be

M. G. del.

Etch'd. by James Storer.

S W View of the Government House, Calcutta.

Publish'd by Constable & Co. Edinburgh July 1.1812.

more commodious at Calcutta than at either of the other presidencies, and in general they wear fewer ornaments than on the Mahratta coast, though in other respects they appear richer and more at their ease.

Of the public buildings of Calcutta, the government-house, built by Lord Wellesley, is the most remarkable. The lower story forms a rustic basement, with arcades to the building, which is Ionic. On the north side there is a handsome portico, with a flight of steps, under which carriages drive to the entrance; and on the south there is a circular colonnade with a dome. The four wings, one at each corner of the body of the building, are connected with it by circular passages, so long as to secure their enjoying the air all around, from whichever quarter the wind blows. These wings contain all the private apartments; and in the north-east angle is the council-room, decorated, like the family breakfast and dinner rooms, with portraits. The centre of the house is given up to two rooms, the finest I have seen. The lowest is paved with dark grey marble, and supported by Doric columns of chunam, which one would take for Parian marble. Above the hall is the ball-room, floored with dark polished wood, and supported by Ionic pillars of white chunam. Both these fine rooms are lighted by a profusion of cut-glass lustres suspended from the painted ceilings, where an excellent taste is displayed in the decorations.

Besides the government-house, the public buildings are, a town-house, which promises to be handsome when finished, the court-house, a good-looking building, and two churches, the largest of which has a fine portico, and both have handsome spires. The hospital and jail are to the south of the town, on that part of the esplanade called the course, where all the equipages of Calcutta assemble every evening, as those of Madras do on the Mount Road. The houses now occupied by the orphan schools being ruinous, there are handsome designs for erecting new ones. The writers buildings, to the north of the government-house, look like a shabby hospital, or poors-house; these contain apartments for the writers newly come from Britain, and who are students at the college of Fort-William, which is in the centre of the buildings, and contains nothing but some lecture-rooms. At stated seasons general examinations take place at the college, and public disputations are held by the students in Persian, Hindui, and Bengalee, in the government-house, in presence of the governor-general, who usually makes a speech on the occasion, setting forth the advantages of the college, the anxiety he feels for its success, the liberality of the Company with respect to it and the college at Hertford, blaming the slothful in general, but commending the diligent by name, and medals are distributed to such as have distinguished themselves. For my part, as I do not understand these languages, I amused myself during the time of one of these disputations at which I was present, with observing the various figures among the auditors. All the college and private moonshis were present, with all the native and foreign eastern merchants who pretend to any learning, and crowds of Europeans. The most singular figure of this motley groupe was a Malay moonshi, whom Dr Leyden had brought to the assembly. A few days afterwards I received from Dr L. a curious paper, containing an account of the Malay's visit to the palace, and of all he had seen there, written by himself, and translated by Dr Leyden *. Ibrahim's representation of the country, the buildings, the people, and the customs of the English in Bengal, looks almost like a

* See Appendix.

caricature on travellers, representations of new countries and customs; but poor Ibrahim, though the most learned of the Malays, has no taste of European literature, so that the satire being unintentional, is the more severe.

Calcutta, like London, is a small town of itself, but its suburbs swell it to a prodigious city, peopled by inhabitants from every country in the world. Chinese and Frenchmen, Persians and Germans, Arabs and Spaniards, Americans and Portuguese, Jews and Dutchmen, are seen mixing with the Hindoos and English, the original inhabitants and the actual possessors of the country. This mixture of nations ought, I think, to weaken national prejudices; but, among the English at least, the effect seems diametrically opposite. Every Briton appears to pride himself on being outrageously a John Bull; but I believe it is more in the manner than in the matter, for in all serious affairs and questions of justice, every man is, as he ought to be, on a footing.

Oct. 30.—I was spending a few hours yesterday with Mrs M. an accomplished and agreeable, as well as a very beautiful woman. I know of no place where I am better pleased to spend my mornings than in her dressing-room. She possesses excellent talents, which she carefully cultivates, a lively and engaging manner, much discrimination of character, a turn for description, and an acute perception of the ridiculous, but which never degenerates into ill-natured satire. When I am with her, our conversation most frequently turns on England. Every new book that reaches us, every poem, especially if it recal the legends of our native land, is an object of discussion and interest beyond what I could have thought possible, till I felt in a foreign country how dear every thing becomes that awakens those powerful associations,

> " Entwined with every tender tie,
> Memorials dear of youth and infancy."

Yesterday Mrs M. gave me the following little poem, translated from the Sanscrit by the late Mr Paterson. It is a description of one of the *Raguis*, mythological nymphs, who, in conjunction with the *Ragos*, or male genii of music, preside over the musical expressions of the passions.

GUNCARRI RAGUI.

GUNCARRI mourns in misery supreme,
Forsaken love and faithless man her theme;
Wild as her speech, distracted as her mind,
And like her roving fancy unconfin'd.
Her hollow eye, her daily wasting cheek,
The inward fever of her soul bespeak.
Despair hath mark'd the victim for her own,
And made the ruins of her heart his throne:
Loose to the wind her ebon tresses flow,
And every look participates her woe.
On a shrunk chaplet of neglected flow'rs,
In pensive grief she counts the weary hours;
And as her fond imagination strays
O'er the past pleasures of once happy days,
She bends on vacancy her sleepless eyes,
And memory bids the pearls of sorrow rise.
Scenes of delight, and soothing sounds of mirth,
Serve but to call new anguish into birth.

In vain the soul of melody inspires
The gourded vin, and breathes upon its wires;
Nor dhole nor vin have magic to remove
The hapless torment of rejected love.
Tired of the tedious day's too cheerful light,
She waits impatient the return of night;
Night long expected comes, but comes in vain,
The shadowy gloom but aggravates her pain.
Her wearied soul no transient respite knows,
Broods o'er its grief, and feeds upon its woes:
Silent she mourns, and like a picture wears
The melancholy dignity of tears!

Nov. 1.—Returning last night from my evening's drive, I passed the English burying-ground for the first time. There are many acres covered so thick with columns, urns, and obelisks, that there scarcely seems to be room for another · it is like a city of the dead; it extends on both sides of the road, and you see nothing beyond it; and the greater number of those buried here are under five-and-twenty years of age! It is a painful reflection, yet one that forces itself upon the mind, to consider the number of young men cut off in the first two or three years residence in this climate. How many, accustomed in every trifling illness to the tender solicitude of parents, of brothers, and of sisters, have died here alone, and been mourned by strangers! I do not know why, but it seems more sad to die in a foreign land than at home; and it is a superstition common to all, to wish their ashes to mingle with their native soil.

Barrackpore, Nov. 20.—It is delightful to be once more in the country, and to be able to ramble about at all hours without restraint; and the weather is now so cool, that one really enjoys a walk. We came here a few days ago by water, and I was charmed with the scenery on the river. Close to Calcutta, it is the busiest scene one can imagine; crowded with ships and boats of every form,—here a fine English East Indiaman, there a grab or a dow from Arabia, or a proa from the eastern islands. On one side the picturesque boats of the natives, with their floating huts; on the other the bolios and pleasure-boats of the English, with their sides of green and gold, and silken streamers. As we came up the river, the scene became more quiet, but not less beautiful. The trees grow into the water, and half hide the pagodas and villages with which the banks of the river are covered on both sides. It was late ere we arrived here, and some of the pagodas were already illuminated for a festival; fire-works, of which the natives are very fond, were playing on the shore, and here and there the red flame of the funeral fires under the dark trees threw a melancholy glare on the water. When we came to the port of Barrackpore, the tamarind, acacia, and peepil trees, through whose branches the moon threw her flickering beams on the river, seemed to hang over our heads, and formed a strong contrast to the white buildings of Serampore, which shone on the opposite shore. We landed at the palace begun by the Marquis Wellesley, but discontinued by the frugality of the Indian Company; its unfinished arches shewed by the moon-light like an ancient ruin, and completed the beauty of the scenery.

The old village of Achanock stood on the ground which the port of Barrackpore now occupies; and the irregularities occasioned by the ruins have been improved into little knolls and dells, which in this extremely flat country pass for hill and dale. A little *nulla* or rivulet supplies several fine tanks in the park, which embellish the scenery, and furnish food for a number of curious aquatic birds kept in the menagerie. The pelican, whose large pouch contains such an abundant supply of food, the produce of her fishing for her young; the syrus, or sarasa, a species of stork, whose body is of a delicate grey colour, and whose head, which he carries above five feet from the ground, is of a brilliant scarlet, shading off to the pure white of his long taper neck; and the flamingo, whose bill and wings are of the brightest rose-colour, while the rest of his plumage is white as snow,—are the most beautiful of those who seek their food in the water. Among their fellow-prisoners are the ostrich, whose black and white plumes attract the avarice of the hunter; the cassowary, whose stiff hard feathers appear like black hair; and the Java pigeon, of the size of a young turkey, shaped and coloured like a pigeon, with a fan-like crest, which glitters in the sun like the rainbow.

The quadrupeds in the menagerie are only two royal tigers, and two bears, one a very large animal, precisely like the bears of Europe; the other was brought here from Chittagong, where it is called the wild dog. His head is shaped like that of a dog, but bare and red about the muzzle; his paws are like those of the common bear, but his coat is short and smooth; he refuses to eat any kind of vegetable food, which the large bear prefers to flesh, and is altogether the most ferocious creature I ever saw.

Nov. 25.—The north winds are now so cold, that I find it necessary to wrap up in a shawl and fur tippet when I take my morning's ride upon one of the governor-general's elephants, from whose back I yesterday saw the Barrackpore hounds throw off in chase of a jackall; but here, as at Poonah, the hunters usually return from the field before nine o'clock. The other day, in going through a small bazar near one of the park gates, I saw five ruinous temples to Maha Deo, and one in rather a better state to Kali. As I had never been in a pagoda dedicated to her by that name, I procured admittance for a rupee. Her figure is of brass, riding on a strange form that passes here for a lion, with a lotus in the place of a saddle. Her countenance is terrific; her four hands are armed with destructive weapons, and before her is a round stone sprinkled with red dust. The sacrificial utensils are mostly of brass; but I observed a ladle, two lamps, and a bell of silver; the handle of the bell was a figure of the goddess herself. The open temple in the square area of the pagoda has been very elegant, but is now falling into ruin, as are the priests houses and every thing around, except the ghaut, or flight of steps leading to the river, which is handsome and in good repair.

There is something in the scenery of this place that reminds me of the beauty of the banks of the Thames; the same verdure, the same rich foliage, the same majestic body of water; here are even villas too along the banks: but the village and the cottage are wanting, whose inhabitants cannot suffer oppression unredressed, and to whom every employment is open of which their minds are capable, or their hearts ambitious enough to undertake. Perhaps there is something of pride in the pity I cannot help feeling for the lower Hindoos, who seem so resigned to all that I call evils in life. Yet I feel degraded, when, seeing them half-clothed, half-fed, covered with loathsome disease, I ask how they came into this state, and what could amend it, they answer, "It is the custom;"—"it belongs to their caste to bear this;"—and they never attempt to overstep the boundaries which confine them to it!

Calcutta, Nov. 30.—As Barrackpore is only sixteen miles from Calcutta, I find little difficulty in going from one place to the other, when either business or the prospect of amusement induces me to leave the country for this place. I came here just now in order to go to the botanical garden, where I went yesterday with my friend Dr Fleming, who introduced me to Dr Roxburgh and his family, with whom we breakfasted. Before breakfast we walked round the garden, and I was delighted with the order and neatness of every part, as well as with the great collection of plants from every quarter of the globe. The first that attracted my attention was a banian tree, whose branches Dr Roxburgh has clothed with the numerous parasite plants of the climate, which adorn its rough bark with the gayest colours and most elegant forms. In another part of the garden the giant mimosa spreads its long arms over a wider surface than any tree, except the banian, that I remember to have seen. The Adamsonia, whose monstrous warty trunk, of soft useless wood, is crowned with a few ragged branches and palmated leaves, seems to have been placed here as a contrast to the beautiful plants that surround it. Among the immense collection of palms, I saw several varieties of the talipot, which I first met with in Ceylon, and the true sago tree. Carefully preserved there is a cajeput, from the leaves of one species of which (Melalucca cajeputi,) the famous cajeput oil is extracted, which is used by the inhabitants of Malacca and the eastern isles, of which the tree is a native, as a sovereign remedy for rheumatisms, swellings, and bruises; the tree resembles a willow, but the bark is ragged, and hangs loose in strings. The garden contains specimens of all the spices, and of the bread-fruit; the latter succeeds worse than any other tree, being usually killed by the cold and damp of the winter. The plant on which the cochineal feeds is placed in the midst of several of its own family, from which, especially the nopaul and the common prickly pear, it seems difficult to distinguish it; but the insect will not be induced to live on any but its own plant. I will only mention one other tree, the Norfolk island pine, which reminds me in every one of its habits of the firs of Northern Europe, but that it seems inclined to grow higher and lighter, which may be the effect of the heat and moisture of this climate.

The botanical garden is beautifully situated on the banks of the Hoogly, and gives the name of Garden-reach to a bend of the river. Above the garden there is an extensive plantation of teak, which is not a native of this part of India, but which thrives well here; and at the end of the plantation are the house and gardens of Sir John Royds, laid out with admirable taste, and containing many specimens of curious plants. After having visited the garden, Dr Roxburgh obligingly allowed me to see his native artists at work, drawing some of the most rare of his botanical treasures; they are the most beautiful and correct delineations of flowers I ever saw. Indeed, the Hindoos excel in all minute works of this kind. I saw in Dr Fleming's possession a drawing, representing the inside of a zenana: the two favourite sultanas are playing at chess; the nurses are sitting round with the children; guards are in waiting, and the apartment opening to a garden, with a mosque in the back-ground, seems to denote that the zenana belongs to a person of distinction. The whole of this picture is finished like an exquisite miniature, and the perspective is admirably preserved.

Dec 5.—We are in the midst of the Calcutta gaieties of the cold season. There are public and private balls and masquerades, besides dinners and parties innumerable. The public rooms are very pretty, but too small for the climate, and for the number of European inhabitants. In three weeks all the gay world will be assembled at Barrackpore, on account of the races, which are run close to the park-gate. This year there will be little sport, as the horses are indifferent, but I am told the scene will be very gay, " with store of ladies, whose bright eyes rain influence." The course at Calcutta is abandoned, as the government discountenances racing, so that it only serves for an evening drive for the inhabitants. Returning from it the other night, after sun-set, I saw some of the trees on the esplanade so covered with the fire-fly, as to appear like pyramids of light. This beautiful little insect is about a fourth of an inch in length; its body and wings are of a dark ash-colour; the luminous part is that immediately under the tail, and occupies about one-third of the body; it is not constantly bright, but the insect seems to have the power of becoming luminous at pleasure. Talking of insects, I must not forget two, of which I saw drawings the other day, the *Meloė cicorëi*, and the *Meloë trianthema*, both of which are excellent substitutes for the Spanish blistering fly, which frequently spoils on the voyage to this country. The first abounds in various districts of Bengal, Berar, and Oude, particularly in the rainy season, during which it is found on the flowers of the cucurbitaceous plants, and also on those of the numerous species of Hibiscus and Sida. The three transverse undulated black bands on its yellow wing-cases, distinguish it from the other species of Meloë. The Meloë trianthema is found in great quantities in the Doab, and the districts on the right of the Jumna. It appears early in the rainy season, generally running on the ground, particularly in fields overrun with the Trianthema decandria; it is sometimes seen feeding in the flowers of the Solanum melosigena. The red orange colour of the abdomen, with the black dot on each of the segments, form its discriminative specific character. The flies should be gathered in the morning or evening, and immediately killed by the steam of boiling vinegar, after which they should be dried by the sun, and put in bottles, to preserve them from moisture.

Barrackpore, Dec. 20, 1810.—I am once more at this charming place, but notwithstanding its beauties, I look anxiously forward to returning to my friends at Madras. The other night, in coming up the river, the first object I saw was a dead body, which had lain long enough in the water to be swollen, and to become buoyant. It floated past our boat, almost white, from being so long in the river, and surrounded by fish; and as we got to the landing-place, I saw two wild dogs tearing another body, from which one of them had just succeeded in separating a thigh-bone, with which he ran growling away. Now, though I am not very anxious as to the manner of disposing of my body, and have very little choice as to whether it is to be eaten by worms or by fishes, I cannot see, without disgust and horror, the dead indecently exposed, and torn and dragged about through streets and villages, by dogs and jackals. Yet such are the daily sights on the banks of the Hoogly. I wish I could say they were the worst; but when a man becomes infirm, or has any dangerous illness, if his relations have the slightest interest in his death, they take him to the banks of the river, set his feet in the water, and, stuffing his ears and mouth with mud, leave him to perish, which he seldom does without a hard struggle; and should the strength of his constitution enable him to survive, he becomes a pariah; he is no longer considered as belonging to his family or children, and can have no interest in his own fortune or goods. About thirty miles from Calcutta, there is a village under the protection of government, entirely peopled by these poor outcasts, the number of whom is incredible.

The Danish town of Serampore is immediately opposite to Barrackpore. It is now in the hands of the English, and is the great resort of the missionaries, under whose direction there is a press where the scriptures have been printed in all the eastern languages. Many other books have also been published under their direction, one of the most curious of which is the works of Confucius*, in

* The first volume of these works is already published; it contains the *Lun Gnee*, a collection of the precepts of the sage Chee. The second chapter of the fifth book contains anecdotes of the daily conduct of that philosopher. In it his appearance, his dress, his words, and his motions, are carefully recorded by his affectionate pupils. It may be curious to transcribe a few sentences, taken indiscriminately from the Lun Gnee.

Confucius, in the Lun Gnee, is usually called Chee, that being his own name; *Koong*, is that of his father; and *Fhoo*, or *Hoo*, means *great*, *chief*, or *teacher*. Thus *Koong*, *Fhoo*, *Chee*, becomes Confucius in our western languages.

" Chee says, learn and continually practise; is it not delightful?

" Set the highest value on faithfulness and sincerity.

" Have no friend unlike yourself.

" Transgressing, you should not fear to return.

" Chung-Chee says, carefully honour the deceased, imitate the ancients; the attach-
" ment of the people will then be great.

" Chee says of governing with equity, that it resembles the north star, which is fix-
" ed, and all the stars surround it.

" Chee says, in governing by legal coercion, in restraining by punishment, the
" people are preserved from open vice; but without ingenuous shame.

" Govern the people with clemency, rule with equity and reason: feeling ashamed,
" the vicious may return to virtue.

the original Chinese, with an English translation, by Mr Marshman, who, without assistance or patronage, has laboured and succeeded in the study of the Chinese language, and in teaching it to his children, so as to enable them to speak and write it correctly at a very early age. To the Lun Gnee Mr Marshman has pre-

"Chee says, observe what a man does. Observe whence his actions proceed. Observe carefully his recreations. How can a man remain concealed?

"Chee says, it is written in the See, respecting filial piety: Only filial piety and affection to brethren are practised in ruling. These, indeed, constitute government. Do not these virtues constitute the real magistrate?

"To behold virtue, without imitation, is of no value.

"Chee says, devoid of a virtuous principle, how can a man observe propriety? Devoid of a virtuous principle, how can a man taste happiness?

"Reason, in the height of joy, teaches moderation. When in a state of mourning, it dictates proper sorrow.

"Of things which are completed speak not; concerning things which are done advise not; past things do not blame.

"Chee says, the father's and the mother's age the son is unable to forget: at one time he is filled with pleasure, at another with fear

"Chee says, I have not yet seen a great mind. Some one replying, said *Sun Chhung*; Chee says, Chhung indeed! He is a slave to his desires; how does he possess an enlarged mind?

"Chee says, knowledge produces pleasure clear as water; complete virtue, happiness solid as a mountain; knowledge pervades all things; virtue is tranquil and happy; knowledge is delight; virtue is long life.

"Chee says, firmly fix your mind in the path of virtue. Constantly advance in virtuous habits. Acquaint yourself with perfect virtue. Be attentive to outward accomplishments.

"Chee says, in the middle the exact point consists rectitude; to arrive at this is the great object; among men how few long remain there.

"Without virtue, riches and honour seem like the passing cloud."

fixed a dissertation on the language, which appears to me so curious and interesting, that I cannot resist making an abstract of it.

The two hundred and fourteen elementary characters of the Chinese consist of strong, linear, and angular strokes, which advance in number from one to fifty-two; both the round and oval forms are excluded. These include the most remarkable objects of nature, as the sun, moon, and earth; the principal parts of a house, as roof, door; the utensils for daily purposes, as knife, spoon; domestic animals, grain, pulse, and the primary relations, as father, mother, son, daughter. There are among these likewise, characters for the soul, and for articles of worship, for ships, and for weapons; a few also are expressive of qualities, as great, good, dark, white, high, long. A few actions are expressed by primary characters, as to run, to walk, to stop, to lead, to arrive. The other characters in the language are formed by the union of two or more significant characters, in order to express a third idea; thus, *tan*, to fear, is formed of three symbols; *sum*, the heart, *sin*, trembling, and *pee*, empty,—an admirable hieroglyphic for fear. But it is singular that, with the power of forming such combinations in writing, the Chinese should never have thought of using the signs as syllables, and pronouncing them; instead of which, they invent a new monosyllable, often differing from one with a meaning diametrically opposite only in the intonation, for every new combination of characters. I can therefore understand, what I have hitherto regarded as a kind of miracle, that the most accomplished scholar might pass his whole life in the study of the Chinese, and yet not be acquainted with all the characters; it is as if a learned European should consult a lexicon for a word, though he knows the letters, with this difference, that the European pronounces the word he does not understand; while the Chinese understands the symbols, but cannot pronounce the word.

The Chinese have no sound comprehending the letters R, B, G, or D, and there are only twelve final sounds which are either vowels or nasals. Respecting the grammar, it appears very simple; all the words are indeclineable; number is expressed by a numerical adjective; gender is constituted by the nature of the object spoken of, though they sometimes talk of a *male man*, and a *female man*. A few prepositive characters mark the cases, and the adjectives have neither number, case, nor gender. The comparative degree is expressed by *kno*, to pass beyond, and there is scarcely a trace of the superlative. The pronouns are of all numbers, and of all genders. The modes of verbs are expressed with tolerable accuracy, by auxiliary characters. The past tense is usually determined by its connection with the rest of the sentence, but is sometimes expressed by a particular character; and the futures by different auxiliaries; the substantive verb is imperfect.

The characters of the Chinese seem to form the intermediate step between hieroglyphic and alphabetical writing; but I cannot persuade myself, as Mr Marshman seems to have done, that they are better adapted for general intercourse than the latter. Do not imagine that I intend to become a pupil of Mr Marshman's, for though I admire many of the maxims of the great Chinese sage, I hardly think it would be worth while to take much pains to become more intimately acquainted with a people, whose morality consists in ceremony,—whose wisdom is finesse,—and whose arts and literature have been at a stand these thousand years. A very curious picture of the private life of the Chinese is contained in a little novel, called, Han Kion Choan, or the pleasing history, published in English in 1761, I forget by whom. It was lent me by my friend

M.G. del.

Etch'd by James Storer.

Fort William Calcutta.

Pub^d by A. Constable & Co. Edinburgh, June 1, 1812.

Dr Leyden *, who assures me it is genuine. It contains the adventures of the Fair Shuey-Ping-Sing, and her different stratagems to escape from an unworthy lover, which of course succeed, and she is married to the hero of the piece, the whole being conducted without one word of sentiment, but abundance of propriety and finesse.

H. M. S. Fox, Kedgeree, Dec. 26, 1810.—I embarked at Calcutta on the 23d, on board a pilot's schooner, which should have proceeded immediately to this place; but by some accident we were detained till the next day opposite to Fort-William, and had full leisure to admire it, as the setting sun gilded its long lines and the white barracks within. Nothing can be more beautiful than both the outside and inside of Fort-William. The barracks are all very handsome buildings, and the trees in the different squares make the whole delightfully cool. There are no private houses within the fort, and the public-buildings seem all in excellent order. I was particularly pleased with the foundery and the machine for boring guns, which I had never seen before. There is a private dock-yard nearly opposite to Fort-William, and another a mile below it, on the same side of the river. On losing sight of Calcutta, I could not help regretting some very kind friends, and many agreeable acquaintance I had made during my stay there; but I hope in Britain to renew my inter-

* Dr Leyden fell a victim to the climate of Java, where he died soon after the reduction of that island in 1811. No person had ever carried their researches so far with respect to the various dialects of India, and their connection with each other. In him oriental learning lost one of her brightest ornaments.

course with some of them, to whom it must be agreeable, as it will remind them of their own kindness to a stranger.

Kedgeree is about half way between Calcutta and Sangor, where the Hoogly widens to a bason, which forms the harbour. Here is a bazar and village, where a Company's naval officer is stationed, who makes a daily report to government of the ships arriving in and sailing out of the river. It is not uncommon for ships to lie here a long time in the rainy season, when the tides are not strong enough to influence the river against the *freshes* or floods occasioned by the rains. Men-of-war seldom go higher up the river, unless for repairs. A little farther towards the mouth of the river is Diamond-harbour, an unhealthy station, and which has none of the conveniences of Kedgeree. But the tide is turned, the wind fair, and the anchor up, and I must go on deck and walk to warm myself, for the north winds are still so strong as to make it disagreeably cold on the water, even at mid-day.

Jan. 5, *at Sea.*—We were near enough to Madras on the 30th of December to see ships in the roads, which must be part of the fleet returned from the Mauritius, where they had not only to take possession of the island, so long the retreat of the plunderers of our Indian fleets, but to avenge the loss of our frigates, and officers and men, at the Isle de Passe. But it came on to blow so hard, that we found it impossible to approach the roads, and accordingly stood out to sea, with a considerable leak in our ship, and her foremast so frail, that we were afraid to set much sail on it. However, after some days of most uncomfortable pitching and rolling, we are again approaching our port. Those who spend their life on shore, can have no idea of the activity, courage, and presence of mind every day displayed on board ship: there is no moment in which the seriousness of business relaxes, because there is no moment in which self-preservation does not require exertion. When bad weather comes on, when gales are blowing, and seas running which threaten destruction to the vessel, the skilful mariner forgets the danger, and only sees the way to secure his ship; his word seems like fate; the slightest alteration in the setting of a sail, a single turn of the wheel, seems to baffle the storm, and to lay all quiet around.

The weather is now moderate, and I trust that the last gale of the stormy monsoon is over for this year. We shall probably land to-morrow, which will be at least a month earlier than any merchant-ship will reach Madras from Bengal.

Madras, Jan. 12, 1811.—On arriving here on the sixth of this month, I found, with the account of the surrender of the Isle of France, a summons to return to England by the first opportunity; and I shall employ the interval in a visit to the ancient and curious town of Mahaballipooram, commonly known to Europeans by the name of the Seven Pagodas, for which place I mean to set off to-night at nine o'clock, so that we shall arrive there by sunrise, as the distance is only thirty-six miles.

Mahaballipooram, Jan. 13.—We arrived here at seven o'clock this morning, having rested our Bhoïs at Tripatoor, where there is a large and very sacred pagoda, and a handsome choultry, neither of which I saw, as it was midnight when we stopped there. I am told that, in digging for wells at Tripatoor, beds of shells have been discovered at a great depth below the level of the sea. I slept the greatest part of the way, and at day-light arrived in a flat uninteresting country. We soon entered a little wood, which brought us to the rocks of Mahaballipooram, after crossing a little river, or rather branch of the sea, one mouth of which is at Covelong, five miles from Madras, and the other near Sadrass, so that the space between is insulated, but the water is always fordable. On our arrival here we found our tents pitched about half a mile from the village, on a little sandy promontory, terminated by a curious ruined pagoda, where we enjoy the sea-breeze in perfection. I found here a Bramin named Sreenavassie, a servant of Lieutenant-Colonel Colin Mackenzie (whose antiquarian researches are so well known,) with a note from that gentleman, who had previously furnished me with a plan of the village, begging me to make use of the Bramin as a guide. Sreenavassie being a Vistoo Bramin, to which sect all those of Mahaballipooram belong, was of the greatest use in procuring information on the spot; and having attended his master on several expeditions to this village, he was the best guide I could have had to all that is worthy of remark in the neighbourhood.

After breakfast I went to examine the ruined temple, which, ancient and dilapidated as it is, appears to have been formed of the fragments of still older buildings. It is said by the Bramins to have been dedicated to Vishnu Narrayn, and to have been destroyed during the religious quarrels between the followers of Vishnu and Siva, when the Stala Puranas were thrown into the sea by the Saivas. A gigantic statue of Vishnu Narrayn lies neglected in one corner of the Viranda of the temple, in the two chambers of which there are square tablets, with figures in high relief, representing Siva and Parvati seated, with high caps, and Brahma and Vishnu in the back-ground. The chamber next the sea has the remains of a gigantic symbol of Maha Deo, of black polished stone, so that to whatever deity the pagoda was originally dedicated, the worshippers of Siva must have possessed it for a time.

There is a tradition, that a large city, and five magnificent pagodas, have been swallowed up at this place by the sea; the ruined temple I have mentioned, and one still entire in the village, making the seven pagodas whence the place had its name. The pillar for illuminating on festivals, and the eastern steps of the temple, are nearly covered when the tide is high; a remarkable fragment of rock, hollowed near the top, and having in the niche a figure, is now only accessible at low water; and, about two years ago, Colonel Mackenzie discovered in the sand of the beach, two miles north from Mahvellipoor *, a number of coins, beads, bracelets, and other articles of that kind, which induced him to believe that there had been a manufactory of these articles at that place, and probably a mint. Some coins found in this neighbourhood appear to be Roman, but the legends have not, I think, in any instance, been sufficiently perfect to be legible. Several copper plates have been dug up, on which are inscribed grants of land for the maintenance of the temples, being dated above a thousand years ago, and referring to the sculptured rocks of Mahvellipoor, as being then so ancient, that history gave no account of their origin.

Finding that I can remain here only three days, I braved the heat of the sun, and at two o'clock I walked to the village, where some of the most curious rocks are situated. In passing, I stopped to look at the temple dedicated to Vishnu (here called *Vistoo*,) an elegant building, highly ornamented without, but I was

* So the natives pronounce Mahaballipooram.

not permitted to enter. Immediately in front of the pagoda stands an unfinished building, called a *Goparum*. It is a gateway which, like many others in this part of the country, is unfinished; they are said to have been begun by the Rajah Dhurma, and are therefore called *Royal Goparums*. There are two at this place, the ornaments of which are delicately carved, and fancied with surprising taste and lightness; one is on the top of a hill behind the temple, and not connected with it; the other is before the pagoda, and belongs to it: its beauty is now increased by its being partially covered with the peepil, which, though it often grows to the size of the banian, sometimes creeps, and attaches itself like ivy. Through the goparum, as through an arch of triumph, the figures of the deities are brought on days of festivals, and placed in the *Muntapom* or open temple, to receive the adoration of the people, who are not permitted to enter the great temple, and who have no opportunity of beholding their deity, but those furnished by his public appearance on great occasions. The muntapom at Mahvellipoor, is placed before the goparum; it is supported by four slender and curiously wrought pillars, each consisting of a single stone, the shaft being about twenty-five feet. On these columns rests a small dome covered with carved work; and by way of basement to the pillars, are four flights of four steps, the sides of which are wrought to look like wheels, whence the muntapom is sometimes called a god-carriage. Near the temple is a large and handsome choultry, and around are the houses of the Bramins, of whom there are still upwards of four hundred in this village. Beyond the pagoda, to the westward, is the first sculptured rock; it is a cave or grotto supported by several not inelegant pillars, and on the walls is represented one of the adventures of Christna, the eighth awatar of Vishnu. He is repre-

Topass of Arjoon
Sculptured on the rock at Mahaballipooram
from Col. Mackenzie

sented as supporting on the tip of his little finger the mountain Goverd'hana, to protect his worshippers from the wrath of Indea, who is showering down stones upon them, their flocks, and their herds. This group, especially the cattle, is executed with considerable spirit. Adjoining to this are the other caverns unfinished; and beyond them, about a stone's throw, there is a most extraordinary group. The face of a large rock is carved into above a hundred figures of men and animals, mostly of the natural size, though some are much larger, and some rather smaller, representing the *Tapass of Arjoon* *, or sacred austerities practised by that hero, in order to obtain from Vishnu a celestial weapon, which was to give him power over all his enemies. He is here seen performing his tapass, standing on the tip of his great toe, with his hands above his head, and his eyes and face turned upwards; at his right hand stands Vishnu, four-armed, and between them a dwarf. The rest of the figures to the right and left appear in postures of adoration; among them are birds, monkeys, lions, elephants, and figures partly human, with the legs of beasts, and wings at the hips †.

The five sons of Pandoo (a king of India, of the Chaudra Vumshum, or moon-race,) having lost at play, to their cousin Duryodum, their whole dominions, and being obliged to retire to the forests and wild solitudes for the space of twelve years, they departed with their consort Drawputty, led by the eldest brother the Rajah Dhurm, followed by a troop of Bramins and other holy men. After a number of strange vicissitudes and surprising adventures in the forests, Dhurm appears to have discovered that they could never

* See Appendix for the legend of Arjoon from the Maha Barut.

† See the Plate of the Tapass of Arjoon.

regain their kingdom, unless possessed of the *Pansuputt Astrum*, (a divine weapon,) and he made choice of his brother, the hero Arjoon, on account of his superior prudence and virtue, to obtain it. Arjoon accordingly set out, and, after displaying his courage in several encounters, he reached the mountain of India Keiladree, or the illusions of India. There he performed worship in the three ways; *Mana*, proceeding from the heart in silence; *Vauk*, offered by speech; and *Neyama*, assisted by ceremonies and purifications: he then commenced his tapass, during the first month of which he eat once in four days, during the second once in seven days, during the third once in a fortnight, and in the fourth he lived on the air as his food. This intense piety so interested Vishnu, that he resolved to gratify the hero's wishes; but he first tried his prowess and courage, by appearing as a hostile king; and having forced him to exhaust his weapons, he wrestled with him till they both fell. Satisfied with the hero, Vishnu no longer withheld the heavenly arrow, and immediately all the hosts of the skies, and every living animal, came and did homage to him, and the gods of the eight quarters, each presented him with a divine weapon, with which he returned to his brother, the Rajah Dhurma.

Jan. 14, 1811.—Yesterday evening, accompanied by Sreenavassie, we left our tents to explore the rocks beyond that of the Tapass. After leaving the sandy tract where we are encamped, we went to the village through part of a small picturesque jungle. On the right of the road is a little natural lake, into which the trees and bushes spread themselves, making a thousand varieties in the banks, which are overhung with the peculiar beauties of eastern fields, and a small clump of low plants, from among

M.G. Del.t Etch'd by James Storer

Teer of Arjoon.

Publish'd by A. Constable & Co. Edinburgh July 1. 1812.

which an old twisted date tree rises, forms a little island near the centre of the lake. A little farther on, to the left, is a large tank, the walls of which are just enough decayed to have become picturesque. A ruined muntapom stands in the middle, and on its banks several buildings of the same kind, some partially hid by the trees, and others boldly projecting, with their verdant crowns of peepil or euphorbia. These objects, lighted up by the setting sun, with groups of natives bathing, and cattle grazing on the edge of the tank as we went by, made an enchanting picture. Having passed the Tapass of Arjoon, we came to an entire temple cut out of a mass of solid rock. It is at least thirty feet high; but the accompanying sketch will give a better idea of it than any description can do. It is called the *Teer* * *of Arjoon.* It is now occupied by a black stone statue of Ganesa, called on this coast Pollear. A little farther on, in a cleft which separates the great rock from another, there is a small cave or muntapom, within which Vishnu, in the Varaha awatar, is represented of a size a little larger than the human stature. There are a number of these small caves in the rocks, all of which I propose to visit, if not prevented by the jungle, which grows over the mouths of many of them. In the course of our walk we saw a large round cistern, which some of the Bramins say was used by Drawputty, the wife of Dhurma, to hold her *tyre*, (a dish of milk, sour and curdled,) while she lived in the forests; others call it the cream-pot of Krishna, and point out a large round fragment of rock which stands on the slope of a steep hill, as the butter-ball of the same deity. On the top of the rock, whose face represents the tapass of Arjoon, we found a stone couch, with a lion for a pillow, called

* Teer, a place of religious retirement.

the Rajah Dhurma's lion-throne; close to it is a fine reservoir or bath, beside which a handsome figure lay on the ground, which we set up; and not far from thence is one of the royal goparums, designed with great elegance. By the time we had sufficiently examined these curious objects, the sun had set, and the short twilight of the country but just permitted us to reach our tents before dark, when I was so fatigued, that instead of rising this morning, as I intended, at daybreak, it was seven o'clock before I joined Sreenavassie to go to see some models of temples here called *rutts*, two miles to the south of the village.

These curious models stand in a grove of palmyras, and are partly covered with sand. They give one the idea of beautiful small buildings; but on going close to them, one perceives that they are each of a single block of pale granite. The most northern, which is that nearest to Mahvellipoor, is very plain, square, and hollowed; it is supposed by Colonel Mackenzie to have been a temple to Kali; it is ten feet and three quarters long, and seventeen feet high. The next is likewise square, but very much ornamented with figures and imitations of pinnacles and windows; it is twenty-six feet two inches long, and twenty-five and a half feet high. The third is the largest; in the lower part are virandas round three sides; the whole is cracked through, and a large fragment of the front is broken off. Tradition says that this fracture was occasioned by lightning sent by the gods, to prove their existence to an unbelieving king. The length of this rutt is forty-seven feet, and its height twenty-five and a half. The fourth model is treble-storied, adorned with galleries and figures, terminated with a dome, and is, altogether, a most finished work. It is twenty-seven feet long, and thirty-six feet high. We ascended to the first gallery by a ladder, to examine

M.G. del.   Publish'd by A. Constable & C.o Edinburgh July 22.1812.   Etch'd by James Storer.

The Five Radums.

the figures which the ornaments on the outside of the gallery prevented our seeing from below. They represent the different Hindoo deities, but particularly Vishnu in his several awatars. From this gallery there are steps to ascend to the others, which are in the same stile as the first. On the ground-story there is one of the figures called *Viraj*, which I first saw at Elephanta. These four rutts are in a line from north to south; the fifth is a little to the westward; it is shaped like a horse-shoe, and is I think the most elegant of the whole; on the flat end it has a portico; it is wrought with a double row of pretty pilasters, and has three stories besides the roof, which is rounded. Immediately opposite the small rutt, or temple of Kali, is the figure of a huge lion, six feet and three quarters long; his head is six feet and a half from the sand, in which he is buried to the middle of his legs. It is curious that, in a country where it is often denied that any lions ever existed, the most ancient sculptures should abound with them, and that the name should be familiar in all the legends and histories. Behind the lion is a large elephant; and nearly buried in the sand there is a Nundi. On some of the temples there are inscriptions in a character hitherto not decyphered by Europeans, and which is probably the same with that at Carli and Kenara, having, as nearly as I can remember, the same appearance. Colonel Mackenzie has found a man who reads it so as to pronounce the sounds, but he does not understand the language they express. These singular monuments appear never to have been finished, being surrounded by fragments of stone which seem as if newly chipped off the sculptures. The view of these objects, together with the loneliness of the place, the depth of the sands, and the distant roarings of the ocean, dispose the mind to meditate concerning the short duration of the monuments of human pride.

History is altogether, and fable almost silent, as to the authors of these works of taste and magnificence; they are forgotten, and the memory of the arts which they practised has perished with them. The monuments they have left now adorn a desert, which Nature, as if in scorn of man, seems to pride herself in decking with gay colours, and fresh smells of every delightful shrub and flower, whose Author can never be mistaken.

After breakfast I returned to the five *rutts* or *radums*, of which I made a sketch, and then visited three others in a picturesque spot, about two miles to the westward, which are in the same stile with the five great models, though they are not like any one of them, nor do they resemble each other. I found walking in the sand in the mid-day sun so very fatiguing, that on my return home I was obliged to lie down, and slept till dinner-time, after which I again went to the rocks, where I found a group similar to the tapass blocked out, but none of the figures nearly finished, excepting those of Arjoon and Vishnu. Farther on, there are a number of small caves or muntapoms, and on the top of the rock there is a large fragment, bearing the marks of the chissel, and seeming to have been intended for a teer. In a rocky glen, full of low shrubs, we found a highly-finished muntapom, containing two remarkable pieces of sculpture. The first represents Vishnu Narrayn, sleeping on the serpent Shesha; two figures at his feet are called by the Bramins, Repentance driving away the angel of death, and three kneeling figures below are called the good, by whose prayers punishment, in the shape of two little imps above, is averted. The other group represents Doorga, here called Maha Mordanee. In her character of active virtue, she is employing all her celestial weapons against Maissassoor, the buffalo-headed demon of vice, who is armed with a club. She is eight-handed, and riding on a lion. Each of the compartments containing these figures is fourteen feet and a half in length, and seven feet in height. Directly above the muntapom there is an ancient temple dedicated to Ganesa. Sreenavassie told me, that it had once been consecrated to Maha Deo, but that in the wars between the Saivas and the followers of Vishnu, the idol had been thrown down into the jungle below. With some difficulty I climbed the rock on which this temple stands, but was disappointed, for the steps being demolished, I could only walk round the building, and the footing round it so narrow and slippery, that I more than once expected to fall; however, the beauty of the prospect repaid my labour. The village, with its houses, gardens, and temples, lay between me and the sea; on the other side a ruined temple on the summit of a hill in the fore-ground gave a greater distance to the plain, with its little river, and the western mountains melting in the haze of the setting sun; and over my head the branches of the Euphorbia, which crowns Ganesa's temple, projected in rude angles, from which the many-coloured convolvolus floated in garlands, waving with the sea-breeze.

Jan. 15.—Early this morning I left the tents to walk to a rock which I was told was only two miles off, but I found it nearer four. The way is dreary and desolate, not a shrub nor a tree, nor even a large stone, to rest the eye upon; nothing but deep sand, with here and there a few patches of thick-leaved plants, and the surf beating with violence on the shore. When I arrived at the spot I wished to visit, I found a few stunted Palmyra trees, and two large fragments of rock, one of which is so tall and narrow, that it seems threatening to fall; and the other, about a stone's throw from it, is carved in a grotesque manner. It is twenty-eight feet long and twelve high, and is cracked through unequally. On the largest portion there are nine heads of animals, disposed in an arch; the three in the centre are full-faced, the three on each side in profile: they are called lions heads, but have horns and tusks. Under the arch are three empty niches; that in the middle is the largest, and is supported by two grotesque animals and two dwarfs. The small division of the stone is fancifully decorated with two square niches, in each of which is a sitting figure, and the head and neck of a horse, a great part of which is buried in the sand. I was really fatigued with the length and heat of my walk, having neglected to carry even an umbrella; but some of the party at the tents sent a *tonjon* or open chair, carried like a palankeen, to meet me, and I got into it about a mile and a half from the rock, and slept most comfortably till breakfast; after which I again set out to see the temple of Varaha. It is one of the caverns whose front is walled up, and now used as a temple; it is said to contain a figure of Varaha coloured *green*, an unusual circumstance, for one of Vishnu's names is derived from his *blue* colour. Contrary to my usual experience, I found that even bribes would not induce the Bramins to allow me to go into the temple. It is now partly kept up by an annual donation from the Company, which, however, is far from being an equivalent for the lands formerly set apart for the maintenance of the religious establishments of Mahvellipoor. On the side of the temple there is a very large slab, containing an inscription in old Malabars, of which Colonel Mackenzie has obtained an accurate copy, as well as of some in the village, which cost him considerable pains. He observed in the walls of the large village pagoda several stones at a distance from one another, inscribed with characters, which, placed as they were, had no meaning; however, he caused them to be copied, and joining the whole together, found they made one intelligible inscription, which had been on the wall of some more ancient structure than that of which they now form a part. It is curious that, in the court of this temple to Vishnu, there is a rude altar to Siva, on which I found some withered leaves and flowers, with a cocoa-nut and some limes. Returning from Varaha's cave, I saw smoke issuing from a muntapom, which I had not before observed, and on going to it I found it occupied by some poor people, more than ordinarily timid; they were of small stature, and nearly naked, sitting round a fire cooking. Sreenavassie declined going near them, assuring me they were of too low a caste to be approached. I found they were wood-cutters, who only go into towns and villages, to sell wood and to buy rice; they inhabit the jungles, living under trees, or in the hollows of rocks, so that the deserted caves of Mahvellipoor are palaces to them.

There is a tradition that, during a grievous famine, one of the kings of India residing at his capital, the ancient and famous city of Mahaballipooram, which is now swallowed up by the sea, received certain artificers from the northern countries, with their wives and families, and engaged to feed them, on condition that they employed their talent of cutting and hewing stone to beautify his capital; and they accordingly began to form the rocks into temples and grottoes, and to build pagodas, goparums, and muntapoms, but the famine ceasing, they returned to their own country, and left their work unfinished. It is remarkable that the head-dress of the gods and principal persons, represented in the sculptured rocks at this place, have not the smallest likeness to any used in this part of India, but they extremely resemble those of the countries bordering upon Tartary, and those represented in the cave of Elephanta. The figures of the Bramins and pilgrims are precisely those seen every day at present, from which attention to truth, in some particulars, it is probable that they have been equally exact with regard to others, and have copied in both instances from the life.

I am sorry to observe, that the Madras government has let the rocks of Mahvellipoor by way of stone quarries, and that they are digging the stone so near some of the best executed caves, as to threaten them with destruction, while they leave untouched much stone of the same kind in the neighbourhood of the village.

But it is time to think of our journey back to Madras, which I regret the more, as there are many curious things I have not yet seen, and figures lying in every field. It is worthy of remark, that all the buildings and monuments are consecrated to Vishnu in this place, and that of all his awatars Crishna is that in which he is most honoured, while, on the other side of the peninsula, and in the mountainous districts, the worship of Siva prevails. It is generally believed that the religion of Siva is more ancient than that of Vishnu, which appears to have been introduced after a long series of wars, when the hilly countries served as a retreat to the ancient gods, while those comparatively modern were established in the plains.

Madras, Feb. 1.—I have been highly gratified with the sight of Colonel Mackenzie's collection of Hindoo antiques, and drawings of most of the temples in this part of India. He permitted me to copy some sketches of ancient Hindoo tombs, called by the natives *Pandoo koolis*; for they attribute to the five sons of Pandoo every extraordinary work, of the origin of which they are

Drawn by Major C. — etched by M. Graham.

Indian Cairns — or Pandoo Koolis

ignorant. These bear an extraordinary resemblance to the Druidical vestiges in Europe, in Brittany, Cornwall, Ireland, and Scotland. They are composed of four or more upright stones, forming a chamber, which is sometimes divided, and is covered by a large flat stone. They are often surrounded by circles of smaller stones, and Colonel Mackenzie calls them *Indian cairns ;* for some of them are, in like manner, covered with tumuli, and in many he has found bones, ashes, vases, arms, and even coins. The account given of the tombs, which cover vast plains in Tartary, no longer inhabited nor even visited, but for the sake of the precious metals found in these repositories of the dead, is so similar to the koolies, according to the account of them given by Colonel Mackenzie, and to the barrows and cairns of Britain, that one would be tempted to imagine that there must have existed, between the inhabitants of those remote nations, a connection sufficiently intimate to have transmitted similar customs to their descendants, although their common origin be forgotten.

India, like the nations of Europe, had its minstrels and poets, concerning whom there is the following tradition : At a marriage of Siva and Parvaty, the immortals having exhausted all the amusements then known, wished for something new, when Siva, wiping the drops of sweat from his brow, shook them to earth, upon which the *Bawts*, or bards, immediately sprang up. Grateful for being called into existence, they sang Siva's praise, but so exclusively as to offend Parvaty, who conceived herself entitled to half their homage; she therefore sent them down to earth, commanding them to sing the feats of gods and heroes, in the presence of kings and nobles, and condemning them to a life of wandering and perpetual poverty. One branch of the bawts, calling themselves *Charums*, pretend to derive their origin from the drops of Vishnu's forehead. They are all held sacred, but their condition is conformable to the curse of Parvaty. They eat flesh, and adhere to the ancient Hindoo doctrine, as professed before the reformation of Mundana Misroodoo*: they are often called Batta Rajahs. There is also a tribe of itinerant boxers called *Ihattries*, who perform exercises and games like the ancient Athletæ. They use thirty-two kinds of weapons, the chief of which is the *Vajrar Moostee*, or horn-fist, with which they sometimes arm their hands in boxing. The Ihattries are divided into ten tribes, taking their names from the ten Bramins from whom they pretend to be descended. They exercise in an enclosed place, strewed with red earth, in which they roll themselves, after oiling their bodies. They pretend to have been taught their art by Crishna, whom they worhip as *Batal*, king of demons; they also adore Kali, to whom they yearly sacrifice a sheep, making her figure, on these occasions, of the red earth used in their exercises. In their prayers they do not distinguish Siva from Vishnu. They burn their dead, and their customs resemble those of the Bramins in many particulars, as in the *Voopa Nayanum*, or putting on of the Braminical thread, and the *Vevahom*, or worship of fire on their marriage; but they marry later in life, the men not till the age of twenty, and they permit their widows to contract a second marriage, which the other Hindoos do not. They use great quantities of animal food, abstaining only from the flesh of the cow, and that of unclean animals; they eat with none but Bramins, the pure castes of whom

* *Mundana Misroodoo*, an incarnation of Brahma in the person of a Bramin of Casee, or Benares. He reformed the Hindoo religion, forbidding the sacrifice of cows and horses, and prohibiting marriage with sisters, and eating of the burnt-offerings to the dead. Some have supposed that he was a priest from *Misr*, or Egypt.

refuse to eat with them. Their proper dress is the *Chelladom*, or short drawers, and the casha, or sash.

Feb. 12.—For some weeks past I have neither been out to walk nor ride, nor even to pay a morning visit, without meeting some one who has been engaged in our recent conquests in the Indian Seas. Those who come from the Isle of France say that even St Pierre's charming description hardly does justice to it; and those from Bourbon are full of the praises of that island, which they describe as rich in every vegetable production, and fertile in the extreme, excepting on one side, called the Pays Brulé, where the lava, which appears to have flowed from the crater on the summit, is still bare and barren. When we passed the island in 1809, the haze prevented our seeing any part of it but the summit, and the cloud of smoke issuing from the volcano, which has not erupted violently for some years, though it is constantly emitting smoke and flame. The inhabitants of Bourbon are described as a simple hospitable people. Few of them having been out of the island, they are entirely occupied in farming, and are now so overburdened with produce, from the want of a market, that the dowers given with their daughters in marriage often consist of so many bags of coffee or spices. The natives of the Isle of France are much more like the European French in their external manners, but they are described as profligate and immoral beyond even the vulgar notions of French licentiousness.

The captors of the islands of Banda are not less lavish in their praises of the beautiful scenery of the eastern islands, and the wonders of their coral rocks, and groves of spice, and burning mountains; one of the most remarkable of which, Goonong Appee, was in a violent state of eruption eighteen years ago, when a new promontory was formed at its foot. This mountain forms an island by itself, wooded two-thirds of the way up, and black and bare above; it is always emitting smoke, and often throws out flame with a rumbling noise; its shape is conical, and the base is very narrow. It is separated from *Banda Neira*, a small island well fortified, which was the seat of government, by a narrow strait and forms part of the bason, or harbour of Banda, which is surrounded by it, by Great Banda, and Banda Neira. On the latter island there is a hill not so high as Goonong Appee, but the shape of which is precisely similar.

The governor of Banda, happily for himself*, was killed in defending the fortress of Belgica, when it was stormed by Captains Cole and Kenah. The inhabitants seem perfectly satisfied with their change of masters, as it opens to them a wider market for their commodities; nor do those of Manilla and Amboyna seem less reconciled to us. The native inhabitants of all these islands were Malays, but the Dutch and Spanish settlers have mixed a great deal with them, which has made them only hate one another the more cordially, so that hardly a day passes without robberies and murders.

Feb. 21, 1811, *H. M. S. Barbadoes, at sea.*—The day before yesterday, at twelve o'clock, I went to take leave of Admiral Drury, who had kindly interested himself to procure me a passage home in a frigate. I found assembled in his house the friends with whom I had been living, and all the naval captains on the station, whom he had invited to a collation at my farewell visit.

* The Governor of Amboyna was shot by General Daendaels, for having surrendered that island.

He had often said, that no woman left alone, where he had the command, should have reason to think that he had forgotten that he was a husband and a father : and he acted up to his professions; for, besides the attention he shewed me in collecting my friends around me to take leave, and accompanying me himself to the beach, I found on board stores of every kind, sheep, milch goats, wine, preserves, pickles, fruit, vegetables, in short, everything that could possibly add to the comfort or convenience of a long voyage, and many of the things packed and directed by his own hand. I hardly thought I could have felt so much at leaving India, as I did when I embarked at Madras; but there is something in leaving even a disagreeable place for ever, that makes one sad, without being able to account for it,—much more when that place contains friends with whom one has been in habits of daily intercourse, and from whom one has received kindness. My companions in the cabin are three naval captains, besides Captain Hodgson, who commands the frigate, and all, happily for me, of cheerful tempers. I occupy one quarter of the cabin, and after breakfast I always write or study for three hours, after which I draw, or do needle-work, till dinner-time, when I again read for an hour or two before I take my evening's walk, so that my time will not hang heavy on my hands in fine weather.

Saturday, April 13, 1811, *off Table Land,* 9 *h. A. M.*—Our voyage from Madras has been long and stormy. We had a gale of wind on the 13th of March, another on the 21st, storms off the French islands, and again off Cape St Mary's, and such constant blowing weather, with heavy seas, that we have had half our stern windows closed almost ever since we left Madras. On the 6th of April, being Palm-Sunday, we made the coast of Africa about

St John's river, in south latitude 32° 48′. It blew very hard a contrary wind, and there was a very heavy sea, so that we were obliged to wear the ship every half hour, to keep in the comparatively smooth water along the shore. About the river this country is very beautiful; we approached it several times so near as to see the surf on the beach. The land is high and mountainous; the hills are of the brightest green, diversified with thick woods, which, as we came to the southward, gradually disappeared, though the mountains still retained their beautiful verdure. On the 7th the weather gradually moderated, the sea went down, and we had fine weather; so that though we seemed to have made but little way, the current, which had been checked on the 6th by the contrary wind, returning to its usual course with impetuosity, carried us ninety-three miles to the southward of our reckoning in twenty-four hours. We were then on the bank of *Lagullus*, or *Agulhas*, and expected to have reached the Cape of Good Hope in two days at farthest, but the wind and weather have been so contrary, that we shall be very happy if we get ashore to-night.

April 25, 1811, *off the Cape of Good Hope.*—I have spent ten days very agreeably on shore at Cape-Town, the neatness and beauty, and singular situation of which, immediately at the foot of the Table Mountain, have been so often described.

The English people at the Cape live like the English everywhere, as much in the manner they would do at home as circumstances will permit.

The Dutch colonists in general preserve their ancient simplicity and hospitality. They usually dine at twelve o'clock, and make their principal meal at supper, at eight o'clock. I was delighted with the fine complexions and good-natured unaffected

M. G. del.

Etch'd by James Storer.

Cape Town from the Heer: Graght.

Pub.[d] by A. Constable & Co. Edinburgh. June 1.1821

manners of the young Dutch women, after seeing the pale faces and languid affectation of the British Indians. They generally speak English well, and many of them write it correctly.

Every day, while at the Cape, I rode out in the fine country at the back of the Table Mountain, where many of the English have pleasant country houses, and there are some fine Dutch estates, particularly that of Constantia, where the rich wine of that name is produced. I was particularly delighted with the Hottentot camp, where eight hundred of that savage people have been civilized and taught the arts of society. Before the last taking of the Cape by the British, the Hottentots, embodied as a regiment by the Dutch, were treated rather as public slaves than as soldiers; their only clothing was undressed sheep-skins, or coarse blankets; they were miserably fed, and worse lodged; and the only art they seemed to have practised was the weaving of mats and baskets. Their condition is now widely different; their cantonments have been rebuilt, and they are fed, lodged, and clothed, as well as any peasants I remember to have seen. Their houses, furniture, and clothes, are all of their own manufacture, for they are ingenious and expert at any handicraft for which they have a pattern; they are also fond of music, and readily learn to play on any instrument. The Hottentots are said to have no peculiar notions concerning religion; those at the camp of Wyneberg have become extremely attached to a missionary who lives among them, and who has taught many of them to read and write; they are all his proselytes, and seem to want no qualification, either mental or bodily. All of them speak Dutch, and many of them English. They are orderly and well behaved as soldiers, but the women are given to drinking. They are remarkably honest; and their colonel told me, that, in the five years he has been with them, he never saw one of them take deliberate revenge. Their dispositions are extremely cheerful, and nobody enjoys a droll story more than a Hottentot. At the same time they have a surprising degree of naïvete. A serjeant, with his party, being appointed to guard some French prisoners on their march from Simon's Town to Cape Town, had to cross a rivulet swoln so as to be breast high. He hurried on so as to get across before the prisoners, and made some of his men stand on one side, and some on the other, ordering them to fire on the first Frenchman who should stoop in the water; saying that they were sailors, and lived as well below the water as on land, and if they once got into their own element, they should never see them again.

Their colonel's cottage is close to the parade, on the edge of the hill of Wyneberg; everything in it is of Hottentot workmanship, and even his dress is made by Hottentots: they are all extremely fond of him, and call him father. I have heard many instances of their attachment and attention to him; among others, an anecdote of one of his own servants diverted me. His master observed, for several days, on his breakfast-table, excellent honey in small quantities; he asked whence it came, when the boy answered, he had watched the bee when it came to the garden for flowers, and had followed it to the top of the Table Mountain, and had taken its nest. They seem to possess quickness of sight, and swiftness of foot, in an extraordinary degree, and are extremely active.

A few hundred miles from Cape Town there is a Moravian establishment of Hottentots. Most of the African missionaries, when they go into the interior, collect a tribe of savages round them, who are willing to be baptized, and to pray and sing psalms, as long as the missionary's store of brandy lasts; but when that is done, they return to their native habits, only more wretched, from the artificial wants created by a partial acquaintance with Europeans. The Moravians, on the contrary, instruct their proselytes to sow corn, to rear domestic animals, and to manufacture articles of various kinds, which are brought to Cape Town and sold; and with the produce, coarse stuffs for clothing, and raw materials for the manufactures, are bought *. Having thus laid a foundation for understanding the necessity of moral regulation, by introducing the comforts of society, the Moravians preach Christianity with an incalculable advantage over those blind enthusiasts who, neglecting to prepare their converts for the belief of real Christianity, by shewing them the advantages to be derived from the practice it enjoins, address themselves to their passions and their credulity, and bribe them into baptism, only to leave them in a worse state than that in which they found them.

In riding through the beautiful country at the back of Table-land, I could not help noticing the variety of shrubs and flowers with which it abounds, although this is almost the worst season for them. The only tree indigenous at the Cape is the White-boom (Protea Argentea,) which is very conspicuous from the silvery whiteness o its foliage; it is of quick growth, and is planted for fuel; the bark is used for tanning, and the wood is sometimes used for floors and for common furniture. The Protea Mellifera is a smaller and more beautiful plant, in the bottom of whose calyx there is a fluid resembling honey, sometimes collected and eaten as a sweetmeat. There is also a kind of myrtle, the leaves

* I have in my possession a penknife of very neat workmanship from the Moravian Hottentots village.

of which, when boiled, yield a fat substance, of which I have seen candles, of an agreeable smell and a green colour.

The Dutch have stocked the colony with oak and fir, neither of which arrive at such perfection as in Europe, though the fir thrives so well as to be useful as small spars for ships. It is curious to see the firs of Scotland and Norway, the oak, the myrtle, and the geranium, with the orange, the peach, and the apple, mixing their foliage, their flowers, and their fruits, in the same garden. But the climate is so delightful, that though the tenderest plants require no shelter in the middle of winter, the summer heats are never so great as to prevent one from enjoying all kinds of exercise.

The supplies for the colony are brought from the farms in the interior by the Dutch boors, who, I am sorry to learn, do not grow a third of the corn they might produce, for they have a notion that the colony is prosperous in proportion to the high price of wheat, not in proportion to the quantity they might export, so that, with perhaps the most fertile soil in the world, they buy a great deal of corn from the Americans, and have been more than once reduced almost to famine. It is true, that government requires them to produce a certain quantity of wheat, but they grow as little more as they can help.

All the wheat, maize, barley, oats, butter, cheese, and fruit, are brought to Cape Town in waggons, sometimes drawn by sixteen or twenty oxen, driven by a single Hottentot, who sits in the front of his waggon, and drives all the beasts in hand, with a long whip, with which he contrives to touch the foremost, and which it is great part of a young Hottentot's education to learn to manage with dexterity. Sometimes whole families come down in these waggons, which are fitted up very commodiously within.

The boors are in general a large stout race of men, coarse in their habits and manners, and accused of great cruelty towards their slaves and the natives of the country; a particular tribe of the last, however, often revenge themselves by setting fire to the corn and hay, and killing the cattle, which they never carry away. These wild people are called Boschemen; they are more savage than the Hottentots or the Caffres, living on trees or in caves, and feeding on fruits, roots, and such wild animals as they can shoot with the bow and arrow, the only weapon with which they seem to be acquainted. They are a diminutive race, being seldom, if ever, seen above four feet high, and they are not numerous.

The Dutch in the neighbourhood of the Cape are much more European in their habits; such of their houses as I saw were commodious and well furnished, and their tables were covered with a profusion of good things, and very well cooked. I ate at my friend Mr Clootë's house part of a roasted porcupine, and thought it the best animal food I ever tasted. There is abundance of venison, excellent vegetables, and fine fruit, of which the ladies are expert in making most delicious preserves. Beef and mutton are brought from the inland farms, and are often excellent; the wine which is commonly drank is small and pleasant, and free from the lusciousness of the Constantia; there is also a stronger sort, which improves very much by age, though it never arrives at the excellence of either Sherry or Madeira.

We intended to have left Table Bay on the fourth day after we anchored there, but it came on to blow so hard, that there was no communication between the ship and the shore, so that we were obliged to wait for provisions and water. However, on the twenty-second we got under way, but it fell calm, and we are still in sight of Table Land, indeed almost near enough to see the races, which are running to-day on Green Point, about a mile from Cape Town. The horses are not quite so handsome as those I have been used to see in India, but I am told they are very strong, and have plenty of spirit; they are bred in the interior by the boors.

The height of Table Hill is three thousand five hundred feet; nothing can be more beautiful than its appearance from sea, especially when it is covered with the cloud vulgarly called the devil's table-cloth, which spreads regularly upon its head, descending gradually, of a fleecy whiteness, while the sky above is of the clearest blue. This beautiful appearance is the sign of the approach of a south-east gale of wind, which always occasions a a great sea in the bay, and a swell without, though this indeed at all times exists more or less on the bank of Agulhas, extending on both sides of the Cape to a considerable distance.

May 7, 1811, *at Sea.*—Yesterday morning, shortly after sunrise, we discovered St Helena at no great distance, breaking through a thick haze. The four first days after leaving the Cape, we only reached the latitude of Saldanha Bay, but there we fell in with the trade-wind, which blew so steadily, that we seldom made less than two hundred miles a-day, with the water delightfully smooth.

St Helena lies in the very heart of the south-east trade wind. It is usual, in approaching it, to get into its latitude a few degrees to the eastward, and there to run down the longitude, as the trade-wind, and the current together, render it difficult to beat back, if once a ship passes it. We made it directly in our course, and our observation gives it in 15° 38′ South latitude, and 6° 30′

M.G. del.

Etch'd by James Storer.

St. James' Town, St. Helena.

Publish'd July 1. 1812 by A. Constable & Co. Edinburgh.

West longitude. It was discovered in 1502 by the Portuguese, who sent on shore some domestic animals, but made no settlement. It has been twice in the possession of the Dutch, but appears now too well fortified ever to be taken from us by surprise. The rocky wall of the island is black and bare; the strata of which it is composed are mostly horizontal; some appear to dip a little, and in one place I saw some of a slaty appearance perpendicular. There is a great deal of matter like cinders, mostly black, having here and there yellow and greenish stains, and in some places a glassy appearance; but I could not be very accurate in observing each part, for, although we were close to the land, we sailed too fast by it, there being no anchorage off the island, excepting the roads at St James's Town. We approached from the south-east, and till we saw the flag-staff, we did not perceive any marks of inhabitants; but having reached the flag-staff point, we saw little batteries perched like birds' nests in the rocks, but not a blade of grass, nor any green thing was discernible. When we got abreast of St James's Town, our eyes were regaled with the sight of about fifty trees among the white houses of the town, and their verdure, and the brightness of the buildings, produced the most singular effect, contrasted with the blackness of the rocks, which seem threatening to fall upon them on both sides. We landed about twelve o'clock at the only landing-place in the island, at St James's Town, which reminds me of an English fishing-town; it has a few good houses, some shops of European and Indian articles, where everything is sold very dear, a church, and a play-house. The society is by all accounts miserable enough, and the inhabitants so much at a loss for amusement, as to be divided into parties, who hate one another cordially, and quarrel for ever. The vallies in the interior of the island are said to be extremely fertile and beautiful. The oak and the fir thrive well on the hills, the date and the coco flourish in the town. Here are grapes, peaches, apples, and bananas, with very good vegetables, particularly potatoes, but hitherto the inhabitants have not made the most of the advantages of the soil. However, the present governor has done a great deal for the colony, and has encouraged plantations of all kinds. St Helena is not subject to the violent rains which render tropical climates so uncomfortable during some months in the year: but there are gentle showers, which fertilize the earth and feed the springs, the water of which is excellent. I do not know if they have attempted to make wine here, but they brew very good small beer for the use of the ships which touch at the island. The presence of a fleet fills the measure of St Helenian gaiety so completely, that an islander once expressed her wonder, "if the ladies in London did not feel "very dull when the China fleet leaves the Thames!"

After tiring ourselves with lounging about the town, we came on board, and were under way by eleven o'clock the same night, well pleased to have seen this curious little rock, but never wishing to visit it again.

June 19, 1811. Lat. 45 2′ N. Long. 26° 58′ W.—What a wearisome thing is a calm, especially so near home! And it is now not only calm, but so foggy, that we can hardly see to the end of the bowsprit; it is cold, the thermometer in the cabin standing at sixty-four. The sea has appeared for some days of a dark dirty colour, covered with white specks, and instead of the delicate nautilus, called by the sailors the Portuguese man-of-war, nothing but the common polypus, which we used to call the sea anemone, has been floating round the ship.

The south-east trade-wind brought us to the line, but since that time we have experienced light variable winds. On the thirtieth of May we observed the whole surface of the ocean, as far as we could see, covered with sea-weed. We were then in North lat. 23° 30′, and West long. 37 31′; the weed continued to float for above a week, nearly in the track which is marked in the charts as that of the gulf stream; but during a calm, though we tried for a current, we found none.

June 27.—This morning, at twenty minutes before two o'clock, I heard the officer of the watch call the captain, to inform him that St Agnes's lights in Scilly were in sight. I have not slept since; the Lizard is before me, and in two days at farthest we shall reach Portsmouth. I can hardly keep my eyes off the land, even while I do what is necessary to hasten my getting ashore. You do not know what it is to see one's own seas, and fields, and rocks again. I seem to know every little boat I meet. The figures of the hills, the varied colours of the fields, the village towers and spires, all belong to my own home, and make me forget, in the happiness they seem to promise, all the dangers, and toils, and difficulties, I have encountered since I left them.

And here I close my Journal, well satisfied that this moment is one of the happiest of my life, and unwilling to write more, lest I should have to record a less agreeable termination of my travels.

APPENDIX.

APPENDIX.

No. I.

OF THE SHAH NAMEH OF FIRDOUSI.

The Chevalier D'Ohsson having taken the principal part of his Tableau Historique de l'Orient from the Shah Nameh of Firdousi, gives the following account of that poem in the first part of his interesting work.

" The Shah Nameh is a production of the fourth century of the Hegyra. After the destruction of the Sassanians by the Arab armies, Mensour I. sovereign of Transoxania, was the first Mahomedan prince who made any researches concerning the history of the ancient Persians. Being a lover of science and of letters, he collected such annals as had escaped the devastations of time, in order to form a regular history. The zeal of his Vizir Mamery, seconded him in this laudable undertaking, and the conduct of the work was entrusted to four of the literary men of the country, namely, Seyyak, Yezdan, Khorshid, and Schandar.

" The fragments discovered were chiefly chronicles, each containing the life of one prince. After the assiduous labour of eight years, the work was finished, and dedicated to Mensour, under the name of Shah Nameh, or History of the Shahs. It was in fact an abridgement of the history of ancient Persia from the reign of Keyoumers to that of Yezdegerd III. the last of the Khosrus.

" Some years afterwards, Mensour II. wished to have the Shah Nameh in verse, and Decaïky, a famous poet of that age, consecrated his talents to that work, but left it unfinished at his death; and another Mahomedan prince made it a point of honour to complete it. This was Mahmoud Ghaznevi, the third sultan of the race Ben-sabuktakin, an illustrious prince, who added to the crown of Zabelistan the whole of Persia, and who, A. D. 999, invaded Transoxania, and gave the last blow to the dynasty of the Ben-Samans, its sovereigns. This hero, who was not less the patron of letters than of arms, employed the genius of Firdousi-ibn-Feroukh, the most celebrated poet of the east, in the great work of versifying the Shah Nameh.

" This poem is still esteemed as the most perfect of its kind; it embraces a space of twenty-nine centuries, from Keyoumers to the last Khosru; but it is to be regretted that the chronological order observed previous to the time of Alexander, is as inexact as many of the historical events recorded in it are fabulous. Some of the princes are said to have reigned during three or four centuries, and we can only presume that several Shahs of the same name have been confounded by the compilers of the ancient chronicles. The same thing must have happened with regard to the heroes of ancient Persia, Zal and Rustum, who are said to have lived six centuries; and among the Khacans of Touran, descendants of Feridoun, Afrasiab, the most celebrated of those sovereigns, is fabled to have reigned above three hundred years.

" Notwithstanding the silence of the Greek writers concerning the ancient sovereigns of Persia, we cannot doubt their existence, from the testimony of the literary monuments of all the eastern nations in every age, so that we must regard the ground-work of their history as true, although the episodes be fabulous. These ancient chronicles may in some sort be compared with the mythology of the ancient Greeks. Several of the Shahs, and even the princes, such as Sam, Zal, Rustum, Gouderz, Kiw, &c. are considered as demigods. They are the heroes of the east, who have occupied the imaginations of the poets and the pens of the historians. Their names have been revered in all ages, and there is no work, even on philosophy or morals, which does not mention these ancient Shahs. They are cited continually as models of virtue or of vice, of clemency or of tyranny, of knowledge or of ignorance, of valour or of cowardice, in order to complete the eulogy or the censure of a prince, a minister, or even a simple individual.

" All the eastern sovereigns, and even the Ottoman sultans, in their letters, diplomas, and other public writings, compare themselves to Feridoun, to Menusheher, and to Key Keavous, and even their titles of Khosru, Houmayoon, and Shahriar; which may be compared to those of Cæsar and of Augustus, of Sebastocrator and of Porphyrogenitus, are borrowed from the ancient kings of Persia.

" The work of Firdousi possesses high poetical beauties, and a rich and harmonious style; but it abounds with minute descriptions, frequent repetitions, continual metaphors *, and absurd hyperbole. It is full of moral reflections, chiefly on destiny and fatalism, and on the nothingness and the vicissitudes of human affairs, which the author usually puts into the mouths of the princes, the warriors, the ministers of religion, and the statesmen.

" The heroes never engage in combat without a pompous harangue, displaying their high birth, their valour, and their great achievements. With menaces and invectives, each announces to his adversary defeat,

* Some of these metaphors are however extremely beautiful, such as the following, applied to a ruined city:

" The spider spreads the veil in the palace of the Cæsars,
And the owl stands centinel on the watch-tower of Afrasiab."

shame, and inevitable destruction. '*My mother gave me life only to accomplish thy death.*' '*The robe of honour with which thy sovereign has invested thee, will serve only for thy shroud.*' Such are their ordinary exclamations.

" In the descriptions of the battles, we find abundance of such passages as the following: '*The motion of the armies shook the earth, deranged the course of the stars, and overturned the planetary system.*' '*The march of this multitude of horses raised such whirlwinds of dust, that one of the seven coverings of the earth added a new vault to the seven heavens of the firmament.*' '*The enormous cloud of darts and javelins covered the heavens, absorbed the light of the sun, and plunged the combatants into the dark agonies of fate.*' '*The blood of the slaughtered enemy rose suddenly to a river, so impetuous as to turn mighty mills.*'

" The legends of all remote ages offer to our view dragons, monsters, evil-spirits, and giants, and princes whose chief glory consisted in fighting with, overcoming, and destroying them. We may compare the warlike pictures of ancient Persia to the triumph of Apollo over the serpent Python, to that of Theseus over the minotaur, that of Meleager over the wild boar of Calydon, or those of Hercules over the hydra of Lerna and the centaur Nessus.

" The Shah Nameh, interesting in itself, would be still more so if it developed with greater clearness the progressive steps of the formation of the ancient Peshdadian monarchy; but the carelessness of the poet on this head is carried still farther with respect to whatever concerns the great vassals of that empire, such as the princes of India, Chaldea, Armenia, Iberia, Colchis, Mesopotamia, Asia Minor, Syria, Egypt, and Arabia, and on the political relations between the sovereign and his feudatories, the Shah Nameh touches but slightly. It is the same with regard to the constitution of Ancient Persia, its laws, its public worship, its military state, its finances, its customs, and its manners; but although Firdousi has only noticed the most remarkable historical facts, he has, in tracing these, occasionally thrown considerable light on each of those curious and interesting subjects."

To this account of the Shah Nameh I shall add a sketch of the life of its author, extracted also from the Chevalier D'Ohsson.

" Mahmoud Ghaznevi had committed the charge of the work, (the compilation of the Shah Nameh,) to Anseri, who was admitted to his private friendship, as were all the sages and learned men of his court. Anseri sought and obtained the poets Feroukhy and Asjedy, as his fellow-labourers. The sultan lodged them in one of his pleasure-houses near Ghazna, gave them a pension, and provided them with every thing necessary for their table and their household.

" These acts of generosity in the prince, and the nature of the work in which the poets were employed, were soon noised abroad. Firdousi, a native of Thouss in Khorassan, who had cultivated his poetical talents, still lived in obscurity. Jealous of the fortune of the three great poets of the capital, he gave himself up to the dictates of his ambition, and went to Ghezna in the hope of making himself known, and of partaking in the labours of his brother poets. After many fruitless efforts, either to approach the throne, or to recommend himself to some of the nobles or ministers, he determined to address himself directly to the poets themselves. He appeared at their mansion in a simple and modest dress, and represented himself as one who had serious business with the poets. On being introduced he found them in the garden, having just risen from table. They were a little elevated by wine, and attempted to amuse themselves at the expence of the stranger, who, after a silence of some minutes, complimented them on the distinctions they enjoyed, and expressed a desire to see some part of their work. Astonished at this beginning, the poets gave him some vague answer, and endeavoured civilly to dismiss him, telling him that they received only poets, because they made it a rule to speak among themselves in verse. 'And of what nature are your verses?' said Firdousi, modestly. The three poets smiled, but said, let us satisfy him.. Upon which they each recited a verse, ending in *shen*, of which the following is the sense :—

" *Anseri*,—' The moon is not comparable to thy countenance.

" *Feroukhy*,—' The rose cannot be likened to thy cheeks.

" *Asjedy*.—' There is no shield that can defend us from thy eyes.'

" 'They surpass,' Firdousi harmoniously exclaimed, 'the terrible lance of Kiw, in the battle of Peshen.' The justness of the reply astonished the three poets; they were even humbled to find themselves ignorant of the historical fact alluded to by Firdousi, and which he explained to them with his accustomed modesty.

" Shame and jealousy overcame the three poets; under the appearance of civility, they loaded Firdousi with caresses, sat down again to table, and, after drinking copiously, they retired and left him in the garden.

" Firdousi, on returning to his house, having lost all hope of success, thought only of quitting Ghazna. He went to the mosque, and, absorbed in his reveries, he recited, in the midst of his prayers, some verses analogous to his situation and misfortunes. Chance had placed by his side Mahik, one of the favourites of the Sultan. They entered into conversation, and Firdousi related his adventures and his wishes. Mahik, finding him a man of learning, and a great poet, inquired where he lived, without explaining his intentions, and the same day repeated the conversation to the sultan. Mahmoud Ghaznevi, curious to see Firdousi, sent for him to the palace, and, conversing with him, was enchanted with his erudition, and still more with some verses of his composition. These were compared with what was already written of the Shah Nameh, and their superiority was such, even by the confession of the three writers themselves, who were forced to do justice to the superior talents of the poet of Khorassan, that the sultan gave him the entire charge of the work, promised to give him a golden *ducat**, and, as an earnest

* *Ducat* is the word used by D'Ohsson.

of his liberality, made him valuable presents, in goods, furniture, and jewels.

"Firdousi employed several years in the composition of his work, which consisted of sixty thousand *bites*, or distichs. The day on which he presented it before the throne was celebrated as a festival by the whole court of Ghazna. However, the sultan was not faithful to his promise. As it was a question of sixty thousand pieces of gold, Hassan Meymendy, his vizir, represented the enormity of the sum, and advised him to substitute as many pieces of silver, with the promise of future acts of beneficence. Mahmoud suffered himself to be persuaded, and ordered the proposed sum to be paid to Firdousi. The officer charged with the commission, not finding the poet at his house, followed him to the public baths, where he was performing his lustrations. Firdousi, indignant at the meanness of the proceeding, only received the sum to divide it between the messenger who brought it, the keeper of the bath, and a neighbouring merchant who sold refreshments. On his return home, he wrote some satirical verses against the sultan, and fled immediately to Baghdad, where the Kalif Ahmed IV. received him with distinction.

"Mahmoud Ghaznevi paying less attention to his own injustice, than to the proceedings of the poet, pursued him with his anger. Informed of his escape to Baghdad, he haughtily claimed him, and threatened the Kalif, in case of his refusal, to march to Baghdad, and to trample that metropolis under the feet of his elephants. The Kalif (then under the dominion of the Ben-Boyes), confined his answer to the three letters of the alphabet, which designate the chapter of the elephant in the Koran. This chapter relates the unsuccessful expedition of Ebreh, king of Ethiopia, against Mecca, fifty days before the birth of Mahomet. The Ethiopian prince, whose defeat is regarded as a miracle, was mounted on an elephant. By this ingenious device, the Kalif referred every thing to the divine protection and the decrees of Providence. He, however, persuaded Firdousi to make his peace with so powerful a prince, and to write letters of reconciliation. Firdousi, obedient to the counsels of wisdom, entered into the views of Ahmed, and sent to the sultan an ode full of erudition and philosophy, analogous to his situation. He concluded it by saying, that, relying on the greatness and equity of the hero of Zabelistan, he was going confidently to Thouss, his native country, which had the happiness to be subject, with the rest of Persia, to the throne of Ghazna. This ode, and the letter of the Kalif, produced such an effect on the mind of the sultan, that, ashamed of his conduct towards Firdousi, he deposed his minister, and sent an officer to Thouss with the sixty thousand pieces of gold, some other presents, and a letter replete with favour and kindness. But Firdousi was no more. Scarcely had he arrived at Thouss when he fell a victim to the fatigue of his journey, and the agitations of his mind. He left behind him but one sister, and this virtuous woman accepted the gifts of the sultan, only to employ them according to the intentions of Firdousi. This poet, so celebrated for his literary work, wished to perpetuate his name by some monument consecrated to public utility. He had accordingly destined the liberalities of his prince to repair a bridge over the Oxus, and this noble project his sister executed as a sacred duty."

The Shah Nameh of Firdousi has acquired a celebrity in the east above all other literary productions. Translations and abridgements of it are common in most of the oriental languages; its authority is held sacred by historians; and the itinerant poets and story-tellers chaunt its episodes at the feasts of great men, or in the public places, where the indolent Mussulmans assemble to smoke, and bask in the glories of the setting sun. Firdousi, Anwari *, and Saadi †, are called the princes and fathers of Persian poets, but Firdousi is always placed first. Besides his great work, the Shah Nameh, he is the author of some odes and several satires,

* Anwari is the author of many poems, but his odes are said to be more sublime than those of any of his countrymen.

† Saadi, the author of the *Gulistan* and *Bostan*, with many other works, is one of the most elegant of oriental poets. The following beautiful apologue occurs in the preface to the Gulistan: "One day as I was going to the bath, my friend put into my hand a piece

the most remarkable of which is that against Mahmoud Ghaznevi, mentioned above. While I was in Bombay, I received a valuable and ancient copy of the Shah Nameh, from my friend Sir James Macintosh. It had belonged to Cheragh Ali Khan, the minister of Persia, who died at Tehranu, a few months before the book came into my possession. It is adorned with costly illuminations, and the delicacy and beauty of the pencilling is only equalled by the exquisite correctness of the calligraphy. The whole number of pictures of the subjects of the Shah Nameh are about one hundred and fifty, of which few copies have more than sixty; mine contains fifty-one, most of them in good preservation. They represent the dresses, armour, furniture, weapons, musical instruments, battles, feasts, houses, and gardens of the Persians. Some of the illuminations represent councils, where the king appears seated on a throne under a canopy, surrounded by his nobles on raised seats, in the robes of peace, but generally with a helmet on the head, and in the hand a club, whose head represents that of some animal. The place of assembly is sometimes in the field, sometimes in a hall, painted and gilt, ornamented with flowers, and for the most part having a fountain in the centre. One picture in my Shah Nameh represents a bridal feast. The bride and bridegroom are seated under a canopy; female servants appear holding torches in different parts of the hall, and a troop of minstrels fills up the fore-ground. The instruments are a harp of a simple form, several kinds of guitars, and a tambourine. The figures, horses, and dresses, are extremely laboured, and flowers, and other minute objects, well represented, but the putting together and finishing of the whole, is as far

of scented clay * of such delicious fragrance, that I addressed it, saying, Art thou of musk or ambergris, for thy scent is such that it would recal the spirits of the dead. It answered, I am neither musk nor ambergris, but I was long the companion of the rose, and her charming qualities have infused themselves into me: but for her neighbourhood, I should have been still scentless and disregarded."

* For washing.

from natural, as in the decorations of a missal. Water is constantly painted black; the brightness of the sky, or fire, is represented by gold or silver paint, as in the picture representing prince Syawousche passing through the fiery ordeal, to clear his reputation from the aspersions cast on it by his mother-in-law, the Persian Phædra. The warriors are represented in all their ferocity by the painter, as well as the poet, who scruples not to make them descend from their horses on the field of battle, for the sole purpose of cutting off a vanquished enemy's head, or of putting a noose round his neck, and fastening him to the saddle-tree; and the imagination of the limner seems to have kept pace with that of the author, in sketching the figures of the Dios, or evil genii, who oppose the virtuous heroes of the poem. For the rest, perhaps the Shah Nameh is not so well known as it deserves to be, though it is certainly not to be wished that the public taste should ever be brought to relish greatly this production of wild and inflated genius, while we have among us the literary monuments of ancient Greece and Rome.

No II.

An Account of Bengal, and of a Visit to the Government House, by Ibrahim, the Son of Candu the Merchant.

This is the account of what I, Ibrahim, the son of Candu the merchant, have seen; this is what I have been present at, and a witness to: where is the Malay who has seen the like that I, Ibrahim, the son of Candu, have seen since I arrived in the great country of Bengal!!

How long was I on my passage from the Malay countries, but how much was I rejoiced to see the beauty of Bengal, which shines like the sun on all nations; for this country of Bengal is so large, that were I to walk for three months, I should not reach the end of the stone houses, which are everywhere so high, that I could never see the hills for them;—this accounts for people saying the hills cannot be seen from Bengal. Alas! I have not forgotten the day when I ventured into the bazar, and having no one to direct me, lost the way. How many days was it painful for me to put the soles of my feet to the ground! how rejoiced was I to reach the house of *Tuan* * *Doctor Layten*, and afterward to think of the wonders I had seen!

How perfect and beautiful is the Fort! how exact all its proportions, its four sides, and all its angles! This is a proper fort; but who would suppose it so large, when it can hardly be seen from without? This is a fault; but why should I, Ibrahim, the son of Candu, the poor merchant of Keddah, pretend to give my opinion in this place, all is so wonderful, and much beyond what I before knew? But yet I must describe what I have seen, that Malays may no longer be ignorant of this great country, but be acquainted with all its wonders and all its beau-

* *Tuan* is synonymous with *Sahib*, *Master*, or *Sir*.

ties, so that their hearts may be glad, and they may no longer be ignorant! Inside of the Fort there is a ditch larger than that on the outside, and at the bottom of both it is level and smooth, like unto a mat fresh spread out, and the colour is like that of young paddy; for such is the management of this place, that when the Rajah pleases the water can be let in from the river, and when the rains are heavy, the water can be let out. Within this Fort, which is like a large city, how many are the stone store-houses for arms, for gunpowder, for small-arms, cannon-balls, and every thing required in war; and how many store-houses are there for wine, because there are many white men, and so many sepoys, that who can count them!

It was in this great country, in this country of Bengal, which is in this place called Calcutta,—how many months journey from Penang!—on the fifteenth day of the month of Shaaban, in the year of the Hegyra one thousand two hundred and twenty-five, at the hour of ten in the morning, when all Malays remained in the same state of ignorance as when I left them, that I, Ibrahim, the son of Candu the merchant, went to the palace of the Rajah, with all the great men of the Rajah's court, and was admitted even to the second story, (or rather second heaven.)

How beautiful is this palace, and great its extent,—who can describe it! Who can relate the riches of this country, and, above all, the beauties of the palace! When I entered the great gates, and looked around from my palankeen (for in this country even I, Ibrahim, the son of Candu the merchant, had my palankeen,) and when I beheld the beauty and extent of the compound, the workmanship of the railings, and the noble appearance of the gates, of which there are five, and on the tops of which lions, carved out of stones, as large as life, seem small, and as if they were running without fearing to fall. I thought that I was no longer in the world I had left in the east; but it is fortunate that I was not yet overcome with surprise, and that I lived to see the wonders that were within, and to write this account, that men may know what it is.

When I entered the palace, and my Tuan said, "Ibrahim follow me, don't be afraid,—this is the house of the Rajah, and he is kind to all people, particularly to Malays," my heart was rejoiced; and as I felt above all Malays on this great day, for there were no other Malays here, I plucked up my courage and followed my Tuan, even mixing with other Tuans, of whom there were many on the stairs at the same time, all of them having large black fans in their hands *, and kindness in their looks, for whenever I raised my eyes to any of them they smiled.

The floors of the great hall are of black stone, polished and shining like a mirror, so that I feared to walk on them; and all around, how many transparent lustres and branches for lights were suspended, dazzling and glistening so that I could not look long upon them!

Until I arrived at the second story, the stairs were all of stone, which formed part of the wall, and had no support. I then entered the great hall where all the Tuans were assembled, and every one looked at me; but I, Ibrahim, the son of Candu the merchant, knowing the kindness of my Tuan, and that he would laugh at me if I remained behind a pillar, so that no one could see me, walked about and saw every thing, mixing with the other Tuans: no one spoke to me, but all made room for me when I passed, so much was I distinguished among the people of the court.

The floor of this great room is not of stone, because it is of a dark-coloured wood beautifully polished; and were I to describe all the beauties of this great hall, the splendour of the throne, and all I saw there, I should write what would not be read in three months. My head turned giddy when the Rajah entered; but, as far as I can recollect, I will faithfully describe all that I saw in this beautiful place.

At the end of the hall there is a throne †, superlatively beautiful, supported by four pillars of gold, and having hangings of the colour of blood, enriched with golden fringe; it is beautiful in the extreme, and

* These were the *cocked hats.*

† Rather *canopy.*

the elegance of the drapery is surprising. Within this throne there is a golden chair, with hangings and fringe of gold, in which the Rajah sits when he receives other Rajahs and Vakeels *.

In front of this throne, how many chairs were arranged in rows, and how many couches with white cushions were between the pillars, on each of which there was a stamped paper †, as well as on the couch on which I afterwards sat down; for I, Ibrahim, the son of Candu the merchant, was seated with the other Tuans.

Near the throne, in front of it, there were many gilded chairs, but one of gold was placed in the centre upon the Rajah's carpet, which was beautiful and rich.

When the court was full, and I, Ibrahim, the son of Candu the merchant, was near to the throne, the Rajah entered, and every one moved different ways. But as soon as the Rajah seated himself, the muntries and high officers of state arranged themselves according to their rank.

On that side of the hall which was to the left of the Rajah, and within the pillars, all the wives and family of the Rajah ‡ were arranged in a row one by one; and it is impossible to forget their beauty, for who could look on them without feeling unhappy at heart! And when everybody was seated, and I, Ibrahim, the son of Candu the merchant, on a couch between two pillars, the Rajah looked around from time to time, and often cast his eyes on the ladies,—when I could perceive that his heart was gladdened, for his countenance glowed with satisfaction, giving pleasure to all.

Among all the ladies there were six who were most beautiful, seated in chairs, being pregnant, some two, others six months; but there was one of the wives of the Rajah beautiful to excess, and she was eight months gone with child. She was kind and delightful to look at, of a beautiful small make, and she sat in front of a large pillar, while a Ben-

* Ambassadors. † A printed list of the subjects of the Disputations.

‡ The visitors of the Governor-General.

galee moved a large fan behind her. Whoever gazed on her felt kindness and love, and became unhappy. She resembled Fatima, the wife of I, Ibrahim, the son of Candu the merchant, but she was more beautiful.

It is the custom of this great country, that the wives of the Rajah always sit on the left side of the throne. They have neither diamonds, nor cats-eyes, nor rubies, nor agates; yet they are beautiful, and their dress is bewitching. Some looked tall and others short, but I did not see them stand; they appeared happy, and glistened like fish fresh caught.

Such! proud Bengala's King and court,
Where chiefs and champions brave resort,
With ladies happy, gay, and free,
As fishes in Bengala's sea!

One beauty shone amid the throng,
I mark'd her nose so fair and long,
So fitted to her pretty pole,
Like a nice toad-fish in its hole *.

One beauty small, amid the row,
Did like the fair *Sanangin* show;
None sotter smil'd amid them all;
Small was her mouth, her s tature small,
Her visage blended red and pale,
Her pregnant waist a swelling sail.

Another's face look'd broad and bland,
Like pamflet floundering on the sand †;
Whene'er she turned her piercing stare,
She seemed alert to spring in air.

* In Malay termed kantasa or *toduda-fish*.

† In Malay termed *barval*.

Two more I mark'd in black array,
Like the *salisdick** dark were they;
Their skins, their faces fair and red,
And white the flesh beneath lay hid.

These pretty fish, so blithe and brave,
To see them frisking on the wave!
Were I an angler in the sea,
These fishes were the fish for me!!

Some time after every one was seated, an aged bintara stood up and addressed the Rajah; but I, Ibrahim, the son of Candu the merchant, did not understand him, although I have learnt Arabic. When this bintara had finished his speech, he looked round to all. Two sida-sidas †, who were youths, went each into dark wood cases that had been placed in front of the Rajah, and then began to address and reply to each other. Four times, as the youths became fatigued, they were relieved by others. They spoke in different languages, but not in Malay; therefore I was disappointed, because I could not understand them.

After the Rajah had amused himself with their speaking, and was tired of it, every body stood up, and he gave to each who had spoken titles, and to those who had not, he gave papers, and small packets tied with red string, for red is the English colour. What these packets contained I don't know, but one fell to the ground from the hand of the bintara, and it sounded like metal; it must have been gold or silver, and as large as a dollar. First, the bintara with the green eyes, (for it is the custom that the eldest bintara should have green shades before his eyes, that he may not be dazzled by the greatness of the Rajah, and forget his duty,) brought the books and packets, and delivered them to the bintara with the black bajee ‡, from whose hands the Rajah received them one by one, in order to present them to the youths. The papers glistened, and were beautiful to look at; and they contained much writ-

* The name of a fish of a dark colour.

† The students.

‡ Coat.

ing for the youths to learn against the next time the Rajah might call them together.

When this was over, the Rajah, who had hitherto remained silent, and spoken only by his kind looks and smiles, took from the skirt of his bajec, on the left side, a book; and, after every one had taken his place, and the Bengalees with gold and silver sticks, and some with whisks to keep the flies off, had arranged themselves behind the Rajah, he spoke aloud from the book; and how long did I hear the Rajah's voice! Every one was pleased; but I regretted that it was not in Malay, for who could understand it!

While the Rajah was reading aloud, the sepoys entered from one end of the hall, and marched along, passing the side of the throne, but behind the pillars. The meaning of this custom I do not comprehend, but it was no doubt some compliment to the Rajah, who seemed pleased, and raised his voice while every one stirred.

After the Rajah had finished he got up, because no one sat down any longer, except the ladies, and I followed my Tuan out of the hall; but I did not hear cannon, nor music, nor acclamations, for the English delight in silence.

It was three days after before I could think of, and recollect all I had seen on this great day I write this history, that men may not be ignorant of Bengal, and of the manners and customs of the great Rajah of the English; and it is written at Bengal, by me, Ibrahim, the son of Candu the merchant, in the thirtieth year of my age, and on the day of Khamis, being the twenty-seventh day of the month of Shaaban, and in the year of the flight of the Prophet of God one thousand two hundred and twenty-five.

THIS IS THE END.

No. III.

THE STORY OF KERAAT ARJOON,

*Or the Penance that Arjoon performed to Eswar, on the summit of the stupendous Mountain Indra Keeladree *, as related in the second Adayé of the third Purvum of the Maha Barut, called Arun'ya Parvum : extracted from a Tellinga Manuscript. Illustrated by a Representation of the Story Sculptured on the Rock of Mavellipoorum † ; translated by C. V. Ramasawmy, Bramin, for Major Mackenzie, 3d May* 1808.

THE DEPARTURE OF ARJOON.

ARGUMENT.

At the end of the Dwapar Yug the Pancha-Pandoos (the five sons of Pandoo Rajah), of the Chandra Vumsham (or Moon Race), having lost at play, in the Crutra ‡ Judum, to their cousin Duryodam, the supreme empire (or Yek-chuckra-adee Putty), of all these countries, he obliged them to go into banishment, with their consort Drawputty, into the forests, there to remain in retirement for twelve years, and one year in close seclusion, according to the agreement made by Rajah Dhurm, the

* The mountain of the illusion of Indra.

† See the Plate, page 159.

‡ The celebrated war of the Maha-Bharut, wherein the two families of Cooroo and Pandava contended for the crown of India, arose from this Crutra-Judum. See an account of it in the introduction to the Bagvat Geeta, translated by Mr Wilkins.

eldest of the Pandoos, at the closing of their game, when they had lost all their effects and kingdom.

Rajah Dhurm at first proceeded with his four brethren, his beloved consort, and a numerous * train of faithful followers; and passing through many deep and gloomy forests, they at last, after a long and tedious journey, arrived in the forest of Dwita Vanum, celebrated among the ten famous forests of Bharut-Cundum.

There, while Drawputty bewailed the misfortune they had met, through the guile and wicked stratagem of Duryodum, Rajah-Dhurm held council with his brothers, how to avenge themselves of their powerful enemy as soon as their term of banishment had expired; and resolved to send his second brother Arjoon, whose fortitude and valour was distinguished among the five valiant brethren, to the famous mountain of Indra-Keeladree, to perform Vogra-Tapasu (the most austere species of penance), thereby to obtain the devastrum from the Lord of Devatas. Having thus determined, and Arjoon being instructed in mystical muntrums, by the virtue of which he might attain the way to the divine favour of Eswar, by the permission of his eldest brother Rajah-Dhurm, taking leave of his mourning consort Drowputty, he proceeded thence, unattended and alone, in the direction of the north-east; and after meeting many and various evil demons and holy prophets in his way, he crossed the venerated mountains of Himaleya and Gunda-Madanum, and at last begun to ascend the celebrated and lofty mountain of Indra-Keeladree. Voyuva, the god of the winds, as he proceeded, fanned him with his pleasant breezes, which seemed at times softly to whisper, and at times more loudly to proclaim, "Behold the hero, the conqueror of his cruel adversaries;" while, at the same time, the Poshpa-Vrosty descended in showers from the Anlarechum (the sublime expanse of heaven), upon the astonished Arjoon.

* Upwards of 5000 Yogees and Poorahits, as the traditions relate.

Shortly after, Arjoon beheld an aged (Vroodtha*) Bramin sitting under the shade of a lofty tree, but, though old and emaciated, his countenance was divinely bright. Arjoon, on beholding him, reverently prostrated himself at his feet, and then sat down and reposed by his side. The aged Bramin then said, "Whence come you, whose noble countenance bespeaks benevolence and high birth? Being here, you shall obtain the fruits of all your vows. These are habitations of the self-restrained, the adorers of the supreme. To these dwellings of the Sounta Tapasees may not approach the warriors, the heroes of the Chatreya race, the bearers of the bow and arrow, and of destructive arms." By this discourse did the Lord of Devatas (for it was he himself who assumed the character of an aged Bramin) endeavour to persuade Arjoon to lay his bow and arrows aside; but the prudent and sage hero, with a noble fortitude, resisted the insidious advice to part with his arms, even for a moment. Sahastraah then, pleased with his constancy, and assuming his real form, appeared in all his majesty and said, "Oh! Arjoon, choose what you wish, I shall bestow whatever you desire." Then Arjoon, with closed hands, replied, "Oh, Dava! I desire the Dava-Astrum; graciously bestow this immortal weapon, by your favour." He replied, "What, is it a difficult matter to gratify this boon? Rather ask the Pona Lokum†, and the Davatum." But Arjoon answered, "My chief wish, my fixed desire, is to obtain the divine arrow, and to be avenged of my enemies, who have deeply injured, and disgracefully banished my brethren and myself into the forest. I have now left them in the distant wilds lamenting their disgrace, and have come to obtain these weapons, to avenge their cause." Dev-Indra then took

* This Vroodha Bramin was no other than the Lord of Devatas Raja-Indur himself, who assumed this disguise, to try the fortitude of Arjoon. This is the emaciated figure seen sitting at the foot of the rock of Mavellipoor, and not Drona-Achary, as the Bramins there foolishly say.

† Punya Lokum, literally the world of virtue, or rather the abode of the virtuous in Heaven.

compassion on his distress, and counselled him to go to a suitable place to worship Eswar, by whose favour he would surely obtain the celestial Pausuput-astrum.

Accordingly, Arjoon thence ascended to the highest summit of Hemaleya Purwutt, to perform tapass. There he found a delightful grove, abounding in lofty trees and fragrant shrubs, producing various fruits and flowers, watered by pleasant pools, by sarovaras and purest streams, whereon on the lovely camalas, the water-lily of purest white, and the Calahara of deepest tinge, displayed their brightest hues; and while the celestial hamsa stately swam before his eyes, and the pleasant strains of celestial music reached his ears, the sweet odours of fragrant heavenly flowers and shrubs delighted his smelling organs, and filled him with admiration. He then began his devotion to the Almighty Param-Eswar in the three prescribed modes of Mana*, Vauk†, and Neyama‡.

In this manner he spent the first month in his devotion, taking food only every fourth day. During the second month, he took food every seventh day; in the third month, he ate only once a fortnight; and for the fourth month, with both his arms extended, and lifted up, he stood immoveable, on the large toe of a single leg, inhaling § the air as his only food and sustenance of life. The nearest Rooshees, seeing the severity of his devotion, were astonished, and said among themselves, surely fire will issue from the intense fervour of his tapass, and immediately went and reported what they had seen to Eswar, who was pleased with his piety and devotion, and promised them to grant his desires, ordering them at the same time to retire to their several Asramums.

Then Eswar assumed the garb of a Kerata Yarooka of short arms. Holding a bow and arrow in his hands, he directed all his Bhootums (or demons) to attend him. Some following, and others going on before him, he

* Mana, that species of devotion which proceeds from the heart in profound silence.

† Vauk, devotion offered by the audible effusions of speech.

‡ Neyama, devotion assisted by the ceremonial purifications prescribed by law.

§ Vayoobacha Arig, *i. e.* "eating the wind."

proceeded from his residence into the depth of the forest, with loud cries and noises, as if in pursuit of the chase to kill wild animals and game. At these loud and hard cries the beasts of the forest, alarmed, ran on all sides confusedly, and the birds of the air in flocks and in terror, winged their way in various directions.

Now Eswar, determined to try the courageous mind of Arjoon, sent an evil Rachasa, Mook Asoor, in the shape of a wild boar, to terrify the hero, who, seeing this ferocious animal approach, undismayed instantly prepared to discharge his arrows at him; but the king of the Keratas, following close behind, called out, "Strike not, nor kill my game." But, unmindful of his words, Arjoon discharged a shaft. At the same moment the king of Keratas shot his arrow also at the wild animal. Struck by both the arrows, the boar fell lifeless, and the Rachasa instantly disappeared, resuming his original form. Arjoon surprised, but not appalled, beheld the king of Keratas advancing, surrounded by a numerous host of followers and companions, and a thousand wild, frantic, skipping females *, and demanded of him, "Who art thou? What is the cause of your coming into these sacred retreats †—this forest secluded from all mortals, "and little suited to wild fantastic gambols? How dared you to shoot "your arrows on the boar that was first struck by my shaft, contrary to "the laws of hunting and the chase? I shall instantly put you to death." To this the Kerata king contemptuously laughed and replied, "In vain "in your pride you boast of your courage and valour to me! Such idle "words are vain. I slew the boar; and if you are bold enough to contend "with me in combat, I am ready, and shall crush your boasted strength." Arjoon, enraged by this language, discharged at once a shower of arrows at him. They fell thick as rain, but Eswar received them unmoved, and

* This description of the king of Keratas, attended by these troops of frantic bacchanals, seems to have some resemblance to the invasion of the ancient Indians by Silenus and his frantic troops of female votaries.

† Chitra-vanum, forbidden forest.

instantly concealed them all in his body with great pride, without a single wound appearing. Then Arjoon, observing this, considered in his heart, "Is this Eswar, or is he Cubera, who renders all my sharp ar-" "rows ineffectual? No others have such power; for, lo! my countless" "shafts are all expended in vain on him, as good words are thrown" "away without effect on a senseless man; while a single arrow shot by" "him inflicts on my body the excruciating pangs of innumerable wea-" "pons; but as this mountain is the residence of holy Rooshees, and of" "Devatas, one of them perhaps has assumed the form of the Kerata king." He then once more shot an arrow at him, that remained in his hand, and looking for more into his never-failing quiver, the famous Achayatoonee-rum, the gift of Agnee-hotra, when the famous forest Coundava Vanum was set on fire, he found it void as the empty ocean, when dried at the dissolution of the universe. Arjoon then, in despair, flung at him his Gaandeevum, his celebrated and superb bow, the precious gift of the same Agnee-hotra, but in vain; it did not seem even to touch him. The hero then plucked up wild trees and rugged rocks by strength of his hand, and threw them with fury at his opponent's body, but they all fell harmless on earth that instant; whereupon Arjoon, dreadfully enraged at his disappointment, flew at his opponent, and a dreadful combat was fought, body to body, with clenched fists and sinewy arms. There Arjoon displayed such fortitude and valour as astonished the inhabitants of the forests, and the Devatas from the skies beheld this well-fought combat with admiration and surprise. At length, exhausted by the mutual exertions of hard knocks and furious blows, the combatants fell both spent upon earth.

Then suddenly Eswar arose, highly pleased with the courage and valour of Arjoon, and appeared to him in his true form, manifested by his distinguishing symbols, the Jatas, the Endu-Cula-Dhur, the Trisool in his hand, the Garala-Cont, the Gaja-Chermambur-Dhur, and the Voora-Bhujaga-Bhooshanu, and thus said to him, "O, Arjoon! I am well sa-" "tisfied with your severe devotion, your valour, and your fortitude, and

" shall bestow all your wishes: thou shalt conquer the whole world. " Lo! behold my real form, through thy divine knowledge."

Then Pardha, much pleased, prostrated himself before Eswar, and praised him with all his heart, and, with closed hands and homage, standing before him, said, "Forgive me, Dava,—I knew not thou wert Eswar, but mistook and supposed it was a Kerata I engaged; I humbly entreat thy forgiveness." Then Eswar held up his hands most graciously, and, with a smiling countenance, said, "O, Dhanemjaya! I have forgiven thine error, " and am gratified by thy prowess and boldness; in thy last birth thou wert " the Rajah Rooshee, named Narroodoo, and with the other Narrain, both " resided in the forest of Badarika-Vanum, leading a retired life in devo- " tion for many years, by which you acquired the destructive and sup- " porting power over the world. I concealed thy great bow, Gundeevum, " and the arrows of the Achayatooneerum, by the powers of illusion;— " once already did you formerly conquer the evil Rachasa by this celestial " weapon;—now make known thy utmost desire." Then Arjoon answered and earnestly entreated, " Be pleased, of thy divine grace, to fa- " vour me with the celestial Pausuputt-Astrum, which has long been the " first and most earnest object of my wishes. Armed with that cele- " brated weapon Pausuputt, which destroys the world and multitudes " of mankind at the end of ages,—which has the power of producing nu- " merous Trisools and mortal weapons, shall I conquer innumerable " demons, and every evil spirit, the hostile kings and chiefs Bheeshma, " Curna, and the other heroes that are adverse to our cause."

Then Eswar conferred on him the Pausuputt-Astrum. He instructed him in the mode of reciting the sacred Muntrums, the Japa, the Homa, the Prayogum, and Voopasumhar, saying, " No other Astrum is equal " to this; if you discharge this arrow, on whatever occasion, it will sure- " ly cause the destruction of the whole world; its virtues are mysterious " and unknown even to Indra, to Cubéra, to Varuna, and to Yama." He then blessed him to conquer the whole world with the Pausuputt Astrum, and instantly disappeared.

The Dita, the Daanava, the Yacha, the Rachasa, then perceiving the resplendent weapon, the dread Pausuputt, borne in the hand of Arjoon, were greatly alarmed. At that instant the earth shook, together with the ocean, and its seven celebrated stupendous mountains. At that instant, Indra flew from heaven, with all his followers; with pure heart and great joy, he carried him to his celestial mansion; and the eight Asta Deckagas (the guardians of the eight points of the world), bestowed on him their peculiar celestial weapons, with their good blessing.

1. Indra, king of the Devatas, and the lord of the Orient, himself offered his divine Indrastrum to his beloved son Arjoon.
2. Agnee, the God of Fire, the Commander of the South East, bestowed his fiery arrow, the Agnee-Astrum, on Arjoon.
3. Yama, Commander of the South, granted his death-disposing club, the Dundum, to Arjoon.
4. Nyrootea, God of the South West, offered the Cuntum to the hero.
5. Varuna, the God of the Ocean, and Commander of the West, conferred his watery arrow, called Varunastrum.
6. Voyoova, Lord of Winds, and Commander of the North West, bestowed his windy arrow, the Voyuvastrum.
7. Cubera, the God of Wealth, and Commander of the North, presented his arrow, called the Cuberastrum.
8. Eesaar, Commander of the North East, at the first bestowed his mighty Pausuputt.

There is a curious circumstance in this paper, relating to the ancient manners of the Hindoos. Drawputty appears clearly to have been the wife of *all* the five Pandoos. In Ceylon some of the inhabitants persevere in the custom of making one woman the wife of several, and in Bombay the caste of coppersmiths (as I was informed) have the same usage.

THE END.

proceeded from his residence into the depth of the forest, with loud cries and noises, as if in pursuit of the chase to kill wild animals and game. At these loud and hard cries the beasts of the forest, alarmed, ran on all sides confusedly, and the birds of the air, in flocks and in terror, winged their way in various directions.

Now Eswar, determined to try the courageous mind of Arjoon, sent an evil Rachasa, Mook Asoor, in the shape of a wild boar, to terrify the hero, who, seeing this ferocious animal approach, undismayed instantly prepared to discharge his arrows at him; but the king of the Keratas, following close behind, called out, "Strike not, nor kill my game." But, unmindfull of his words, Arjoon discharged a shaft. At the same moment the king of Keratas shot his arrow also at the wild animal. Struck by both the arrows, the boar fell lifeless, and the Rachasa instantly disappeard, resuming his original form. Arjoon surprised, but not appalled, beheld the king of Keratas advancing, surrounded by a numerous host of followers and companions, and a thousand wild, frantic, skipping females *, and demanded of him, "Who art thou? What is the cause of your coming into these sacred retreats †—this forest secluded from all mortals, and little suited to wild fantastic gambols? How dared you to shoot your arrows on the boar that was first struck by my shaft, contrary to the laws of hunting and the chase? I shall instantly put you to death." To this the Kerata king contemptuously laughed and replied, "In vain in your pride you boast of your courage and valour to me! Such idle words are vain. I slew the boar; and if you are bold enough to contend with me in combat, I am ready, and shall crush your boasted strength." Arjoon, enraged by this language, discharged at once a shower of arrows at him. They fell thick as rain, but Eswar received them unmoved, and

* This description of the king of Keratas, attended by these troops of frantic bacchanals, seems to have some resemblance to the invasion of the ancient Indians by Silenus and his frantic troops of female votaries.

† Chitra-vanum, forbidden forest.

instantly concealed them all in his body with great pride, without a single wound appearing Then Arjoon, observing this, considered in his heart, " Is this Eswar, or is he Cubera, who renders all my sharp ar-
" rows ineffectual? No others have such power; for, lo! my countless
" shafts are all expended in vain on him, as good words are thrown
" away without effect on a senseless man; while a single arrow shot by
" him inflicts on my body the excruciating pangs of innumerable wea-
" pons; but as this mountain is the residence of holy Rooshees, and of
" Devatas, one of them perhaps has assumed the form of the Kerata king."
He then once more shot an arrow at him, that remained in his hand, and looking for more into his never-failing quiver, the famous Achayatooneerum, the gift of Agnee-hotra, when the famous forest Coundava Vanum was set on fire, he found it void as the empty ocean, when dried at the dissolution of the universe. Arjoon then, in despair, flung at him his Gaandeevum, his celebrated and superb bow, the precious gift of the same Agnee-hotra, but in vain; it did not seem even to touch him. The hero then plucked up wild trees and rugged rocks by strength of his hand, and threw them with fury at his opponent's body, but they all fell harmless on earth that instant; whereupon Arjoon, dreadfully enraged at his disappointment, flew at his opponent, and a dreadful combat was fought, body to body, with clenched fists and sinewy arms. There Arjoon displayed such fortitude and valour as astonished the inhabitants of the forests, and the Devatas from the skies beheld this well-fought combat with admiration and surprise. At length, exhausted by the mutual exertions of hard knocks and furious blows, the combatants fell both spent upon earth.

Then suddenly Eswar arose, highly pleased with the courage and valour of Arjoon, and appeared to him in his true form, manifested by his distinguishing symbols, the Jatas, the Endu-Cula-Dhur, the Trisool in his hand, the Garala-Cont, the Gaja Chermambur-Dhur, and the Voora-Bhujaga-Bhooshanu, and thus said to him, " O, Arjoon! I am well sa-
" tisfied with your severe devotion, your valour, and your fortitude, and

"shall bestow all your wishes: thou shalt conquer the whole world. "Lo! behold my real form, through thy divine knowledge."

Then Pardha, much pleased, prostrated himself before Eswar, and praised him with all his heart, and, with closed hands and homage, standing before him, said, "Forgive me, Dava,—I knew not thou wert Eswar, "but mistook and supposed it was a Kerata I engaged; I humbly entreat thy "forgiveness." Then Eswar held up his hands most graciously, and, with a smiling countenance, said, "O, Dhanemjaya! I have forgiven thine error, "and am gratified by thy prowess and boldness; in thy last birth thou wert "the Rajah Rooshee, named Narroodoo, and with the other Narrain, both "resided in the forest of Badarika-Vanum, leading a retired life in devo- "tion for many years, by which you acquired the destructive and sup- "porting power over the world. I concealed thy great bow, Gundeevum, "and the arrows of the Achayatooneerum, by the powers of illusion;— "once already did you formerly conquer the evil Rachasa by this celestial "weapon;—now make known thy utmost desire." Then Arjoon answered and earnestly entreated, "Be pleased, of thy divine grace, to fa- "vour me with the celestial Pausuputt-Astrum, which has long been the "first and most earnest object of my wishes. Armed with that cele- "brated weapon Pausuputt, which destroys the world and multitudes "of mankind at the end of ages,—which has the power of producing nu- "merous Trisools and mortal weapons, shall I conquer innumerable "demons, and every evil spirit, the hostile kings and chiefs Beeshma, "Curna, and the other heroes that are adverse to our cause."

Then Eswar conferred on him the Pausuputt-Astrum. He instructed him in the mode of reciting the sacred Muntrums, the Japa, the Homa, the Prayogum, and Voopasumhar, saying, "No other Astrum is equal "to this; if you discharge this arrow, on whatever occasion, it will sure- "ly cause the destruction of the whole world; its virtues are mysterious "and unknown even to Indra, to Cubera, to Varuna, and to Yama." He then blessed him to conquer the whole world with the Pausuputt-Astrum, and instantly disappeared.

The Dita, the Daanava, the Yacha, the Rachasa, then perceiving the resplendent weapon, the dread Pausuputt, borne in the hand of Arjoon, were greatly alarmed. At that instant the earth shook, together with the ocean, and its seven celebrated stupendous mountains. At that instant, Indra flew from heaven, with all his followers; with pure heart and great joy, he carried him to his celestial mansion; and the eight Asta Deckagas (the guardians of the eight points of the world), bestowed on him their peculiar celestial weapons, with their good blessing.

1. Indra, king of the Devatas, and the lord of the Orient, himself offered his divine Indrastrum to his beloved son Arjoon.

2. Agnee, the God of Fire, the Commander of the South East, bestowed his fiery arrow, the Agnee-Astrum, on Arjoon.

3. Yama, Commander of the South, granted his death-disposing club, the Dundum, to Arjoon.

4. Nyrootea, God of the South West, offered the Cuntum to the hero.

5. Varuna, the God of the Ocean, and Commander of the West, conferred his watery arrow, called Varunastrum.

6. Voyoova, Lord of Winds, and Commander of the North West, bestowed his windy arrow, the Voyuvastrum.

7. Cubera, the God of Wealth, and Commander of the North, presented his arrow, called the Cuberastrum,

8. Eesaar, Commander of the North East, at the first bestowed his mighty Pausuputt.

There is a curious circumstance in this paper, relating to the ancient manners of the Hindoos. Drawputty appears clearly to have been the wife of *all* the five Pandoos. In Ceylon, some of the inhabitants persevere in the custom of making one woman the wife of several, and in Bombay the caste of coppersmiths (as I was informed) have the same usage.

THE END.